GINO'S

ITALIAN FAMILY ADVENTURE

GINO'S

ITALIAN FAMILY ADVENTURE

BLOOMSBURY PUBLISHING
LONDON · OXFORD · NEW YORK · NEW DELHI · SYDNEY

DEDICATION

DEDIZIONE

◆◆◆◆◆◆◆◆◆◆◆◆◆◆◆◆◆◆◆◆◆◆◆◆◆◆◆◆

For my mum Alba and dad Ciro, who were missed more than ever while I was writing this book and filming the show. Their love, laughter, recipes and passion for food will be with me and my family forever.

◆◆◆◆◆◆◆◆◆◆◆◆◆◆◆◆◆◆◆◆◆◆◆◆◆◆◆◆

CONTENTS

CONTENTUI

◆◆◆◆◆◆◆◆◆◆◆◆◆◆◆◆◆◆◆◆◆◆

◆◆◆◆◆◆◆◆◆◆◆◆◆◆◆◆◆◆◆◆◆◆

INTRODUCTION

INTRODUZIONE

◆◆◆◆◆◆◆◆◆◆◆◆◆◆◆◆◆◆◆◆◆◆◆◆◆◆

This is by far the most exciting cookbook I have written, because it's about my family. It's about what we do and what we eat. It's the reality of our lives.

To Italians, nothing is more important than family and food. It's not just a cliché that we think like this, it's completely real. I strongly believe that food is the best way to bring everyone together. We all need to eat, and cooking together and eating around the table are great opportunities to spend some proper time with the people we love.

The recipes in this book are designed to make food fit into your life. It shouldn't be a big deal to eat well. The D'Acampo family is a very happy healthy family and if it's working for us, then it can work for everyone. Most of the recipes are inexpensive, using ingredients you can get anywhere, and they are generally quick to make. There are a few that are a bit more luxurious, but we all deserve a treat sometimes!

The book has really been in the making for the past ten years. I've collected together all the notes, all the little pieces of paper that we have flying around the kitchen of things that we like to cook, and finally written it all down. I can't wait to share it with you.

Live like a king

In Italy, you can live like royalty with very little money. To have a good bond with your family and eat well doesn't cost a lot, and I really believe that is what life is all about. Travelling around the south of Italy for the television series that goes with this book allowed me to share with my family the experiences I had as a young boy growing up there. My children live a very privileged life and it's really important to me that they appreciate their roots and know how lucky they are. I was a little bit nervous to see their reactions to some of the places I shared with them. I grew up in a small house in my little town of Torre del Greco, I had the same push-bike for ten years and I used to go fishing by myself all the time. It was very different from the life I have given them.

◆◆◆◆◆◆◆◆◆◆◆◆◆◆◆◆◆◆◆◆◆◆◆◆◆◆◆◆

I come from a very large family. My mother had nine sisters and one brother and my father had two sisters. When we all got together it was always a big event, at one point we counted sixty-nine cousins! Food has always played a central role. One of my earliest memories is of my grandfather, Nonno Giovanni. He used to be a chef too. I remember like it was yesterday: it was Christmas time and we were in his kitchen. There were about thirty of us round for lunch and he showed me for the first time how to make potato gnocchi. It was something so simple, just potato and flour, a little bit of tomato sauce, fresh basil and Parmesan cheese. Job done. I remember thinking, 'This is pure magic. How can this man take just a handful of ingredients and feed a family of thirty something so delicious?' That moment of realisation has stayed with me and the food I cook has always been very much based on that experience. I believe that you really need to do very little with food to eat well. Get the best ingredients that you can and then let them deliver great flavours. There's no need to do any fancy plating up, Michelin-star style, or mess around with things. To me, that isn't true Italian food.

Real Italian cooking was created by normal working people. They used whatever ingredients were grown locally to them and were in season, and they knew exactly how to put those ingredients together to make something truly delicious. What ingredients were available depended very much on where they lived. The climate and the landscape have a huge impact on how well things grow, and, because of this, the style of Italian food varies a lot depending on where you are in the country.

I'm from the south of Italy, near to Naples, where the weather is warmer. The food tends to be much lighter and fresher. There are a lot of olive groves there, so we use olive oil in our cooking, whereas in the north they tend to use butter because they can keep cows in their cooler climate. In the south we eat a lot of seafood; in the north they eat more meat. The food is also often a bit richer and heavier in the northern areas because it's colder. People are very proud of their local specialities and I'm no different. To me, nothing compares to a tomato grown near Naples, around Mount Vesuvius, it's the best in the world.

◆◆◆◆◆◆◆◆◆◆◆◆◆◆◆◆◆◆◆◆◆◆◆◆◆◆◆◆◆◆

The black soil around the volcano is rich in minerals from the lava, so it grows fantastic vegetables and fruit, while also supplying good grazing for the buffalos that produce milk for the amazing buffalo mozzarella you only find there.

Whenever you eat in Italy, you know you're having ingredients that are in season, when they're at their very best. It's very exciting to me as a chef to work with such beautiful ingredients and it's what still excites me about cooking Italian food today. If you buy seasonal produce, grown as locally as possible, it can make a huge difference to how your food tastes. I feel strongly about this and think we should all be making a bit of an effort to eat more seasonally. What's the point of eating asparagus at Christmas? It won't taste as good and it will cost you more. We should only be buying asparagus in the spring in the UK, and we definitely shouldn't be flying in our fruit and veg from halfway around the world.

Let's all be more Italian

Naples and all the south of Italy have always had a lot of street food. As kids, we'd be out of the house all day and pick up snacks like pizza, croquettes filled with buffalo mozzarella and cooked ham, little pasta and lasagne boxes that we used to get from the bars, and corn on the cob that came from little stands near the beach, which were much better than the candy floss which the same stalls sell now, in my opinion. It's no secret that I didn't go to school all that much. I went to catering college for five years, but I was only really interested in the food, hygiene and business part of the course, so when it was a day of cooking, I was in school, but when it was a day of general studying, I'd be somewhere else. I was very good at cooking though, so the teachers let me get away with it. They understood that I didn't like school and they encouraged me to concentrate on what I was passionate about. I think we can learn a lot from that. There are so many children who don't perform well academically in school and are nevertheless put under so much pressure to reach those high grades.

What we should be doing is helping them to realise what *they* are good at, encouraging what *they* love. It definitely worked for me. I was a bit of a wild child growing up, like everyone else was back then. We didn't have a lot of toys, so we used to play football all the time, mostly in the middle of the roads with the cars going up and down. I even have a photo of me with Maradona! When you're out in the streets you meet a lot of characters and you need to be aware of lots of things, so we were definitely wiser. Looking back, it was quite a dangerous way of living for a child, but I'd say it was also a beautiful one and definitely more interactive than it is today.

I love Italy and that's not only because I'm Italian, I think we all have this romantic idea of Italy having a simpler pace of life. It's what we all love about going on holiday there, as well as the sunshine. It's a more back-to-basics way of life, with a deep connection to history and culture, where everyone spends a lot more time with friends and family, usually sitting outside, away from phones and computers and televisions and always eating good food.

My family and I are lucky to live half the year in the UK and half the year in Sardinia, but even when I'm with my own family in Italy we spend a lot more time with each other, going for walks or just being together outside. It has a lot to do with the climate of course. It's the same in the UK: when the weather is good, we're much more likely to invite people over for a barbecue or have friends round for a party in the garden, or just meet up in the park. I honestly think we all feel better for eating and socialising outside, but don't just take my word for it... Ogliastra in Sardinia is now one of five designated Blue Zones, which are areas of the world where people regularly live to the age of one hundred and beyond! Their long and healthy life is thought to be partly due to the food they eat – grains, dairy, vegetables, olive oil, nuts and just a little bit of meat and fish – along with a special local red wine that is particularly high in antioxidants. Sardinians also surround themselves with friends and family, spend a lot of time in the sunshine and fresh air, and relax. It's everything the Italian good life represents.

◆◆◆◆◆◆◆◆◆◆◆◆◆◆◆◆◆◆◆◆◆◆◆◆◆

So how can we create more of that Italian way of living here in the UK? Unfortunately, I can't bring you the Sardinian sunshine but what I can do is share with you what we do in the south of Italy, and, more importantly, what we eat. Connecting with your family and cooking good food is what will help to recreate that Italian way of life at home, even when it's raining outside. With most of these recipes, I promise you won't need to spend a lot of time in the kitchen, allowing you to focus on the more important job of being with your family or guests.

Prioritise meal times

I know it can sometimes feel like a bit of a battle to get everyone around the table to eat together, but I think it's really important to try and do this whenever you can. In my house, as often as we're able to, everyone sits at the table ten or fifteen minutes before dinner is ready and no one can put on the TV or radio or look at their phones. We all talk with each other. It may sound strict or old-fashioned, but if you ask my children, they will say they are really grateful that I insist we all sit together without any distractions.

So often, I hear about families sitting in different rooms to eat, or eating at different times of the day. If you want to make eating as a family a priority, then you have to make a few rules. I guarantee it will be worth it because everyone will enjoy it, parents can be completely focused on what their kids have to say rather than worrying about work and checking mobiles, and kids will be talking and listening rather than watching TV or playing games. It's such an important and special time. I really recommend you try to do this, even if you can manage it just once a week.

I think it's really important to encourage your children's interest in food from a young age. Luckily, my family are all real foodies. I love spending time with them in the kitchen. One of my favourite things to do is make meatballs with my daughter, Mia, and you'll find our recipe in these pages. If my kids show an interest in a particular ingredient, then we'll make sure to cook something with it.

◆◆◆◆◆◆◆◆◆◆◆◆◆◆◆◆◆◆◆◆◆◆◆◆◆◆◆◆◆

Luciano loves stinky blue cheese, so I use it in one of the risottos that are featured. It's great to get them excited about good food and it will help them to establish a healthy relationship with what they eat. I don't believe children should be given special meals though. When we sit at the table, we all eat the same food. I don't run a restaurant in my house, so whatever my wife or I decide to cook, we put it on the table and that's what we all eat. It's a great way to get kids to try everything and anything from a young age.

Make my recipes work for you

Italy has a hugely long food history going back thousands of years. As a chef, I love to show respect for those ancient traditions, but I like to bring something new to the table too. Certain recipes are so beautiful the way they are that I'll stick to the exact recipe; there's no point changing a dish if it's perfect already. Others, I might give a Gino twist! I love to play around with recipes. Sometimes I can't get hold of the right ingredient, so I'll replace it with something else, or maybe I've raided my fridge and have something I need to use up (I hate to waste food). I also sometimes like to bring in other flavours from around the world, for example I've added Chinese aromatics to sea bream in this book. Other times, I tinker with a recipe because I've drunk a bit too much wine and think I can change a dish… sometimes it works and sometimes it doesn't, but it's all part of the fun. I really encourage you to experiment, too. Just try it!

In these pages you'll find super-Quick recipes that will be on your table in under thirty minutes and One Pot wonders that you can just stick in the oven or on the hob while you get on with life. Then there is a Lighter chapter, with a maximum of five hundred calories per serving. I don't really believe in dieting, but I do believe in balance: Italians love a meal with lots of courses and sometimes we need to rein it in a bit! Sunday Specials are some of my favourite recipes in the book. These are meals we cook as a family when we can all spend some real time together in the kitchen and around the table. It's my favourite

◆◆◆◆◆◆◆◆◆◆◆◆◆◆◆◆◆◆◆◆◆◆◆◆◆

day of the week. My chapter Kids Are Out is a collection of recipes designed for two. Family is not just about the kids and it is important to make time for your partner, whether you've been together for two years or for fifty! To be honest, more often than not, these recipes are for me and one of the kids when everyone else is out for the evening. Rocco and I love to eat steak sandwiches and watch a movie on the sofa together. Last but not least, it wouldn't be a D'Acampo family cookbook without a Desserts chapter; we all have a sweet tooth in our house, so I've included some of our regular after-dinner treats.

With these recipes I want to remind everybody that you can live a beautiful life, eat delicious simple food and enjoy it with your family and friends without being extravagant about it *and* without it feeling like hard work. If as a family you follow what we do, sitting around the table, eating and talking together, then that to me is a winner. This special book is from me and my family to you and your family: let's all be a bit more Italian!

QUICK

◆◆◆◆◆◆◆◆◆◆◆◆◆◆◆◆◆◆◆◆◆◆◆◆◆

Families are getting busier and busier and if your kids are anything like mine, their social life is just as crazy, if not more so, than ours. How many of you have had to whip up a meal super-quickly before going out to work, or taking one of your kids to a football game or ballet class? Those are the times when this chapter is, in my wife Jessica's words, a godsend.

This is good home-cooked food, better, healthier (and cheaper) than any takeaway and not at all time-consuming to create. Don't be fooled by the chapter title into thinking that 'quick' means 'basic', either: there are many recipes here that are perfect to serve at a dinner party, leaving you more time to spend with your guests. Both the salmon tartare and Gorgonzola tartlets are particularly good-looking and will make elegant starters. I'd eat the tagliatelle with mixed seafood every day if it was up to me, while the spinach and Marsala with a ribeye steak is an absolute must-try. If you're in a real rush to head out of the door, the chicken goujon wraps or the tuna patties are great for eating on-the-go by the whole family. We make and love them all!

I realise this is a cookbook, so it might sound a bit odd for me to say this, but if you're completely exhausted and really can't be bothered to cook, then don't. I know that when you feel that way, even with quick options such as these, you should not cook, because the food will never taste that great anyway. Those are the days that takeaways are made for! Food has to be made with love, because it makes it taste so much better.

My family has made, served and eaten all the dishes on the following pages more times over than we could ever count. For those of you who are making food for busy families and have busy lives, I hope they can help you to enjoy cooking again. From me to you… with love.

◆◆◆◆◆◆◆◆◆◆◆◆◆◆◆◆◆◆◆◆◆◆◆◆◆

TRIO OF BRUSCHETTA

BRUSCHETTE MISTE

◆◆◆◆◆◆◆◆◆◆◆◆◆◆◆◆◆◆◆◆◆◆◆◆◆◆◆◆◆

I absolutely love making bruschetta. It's a fantastic opportunity to get creative with the toppings and it is so much fun coming up with new recipes. Most people serve them as an easy starter, which is great, but during the summer I often make a varied selection and they become lunch with a cold beer (obviously my eight-year-old daughter doesn't get the beer). I have chosen three of our favourites for you to try. Serve them immediately once they are made, as you don't want the bread to go soggy.

SERVES 4

12 slices of ciabatta, cut into 1.5cm-thick slices

fine sea salt

SPICY CRAB

200g white crab meat, roughly chopped

3 tsp Tabasco sauce

1 tbsp sweet chilli sauce (tomato ketchup also works)

2 tbsp mayonnaise

4 tsp finely chopped chives

WILD MUSHROOM

4 tbsp olive oil

1 garlic clove, crushed

½ tbsp finely chopped rosemary

100g diced pancetta

300g mixed wild mushrooms, sliced

½ tsp chilli flakes

40g salted butter

30g finely grated Parmesan cheese

TOMATO, GARLIC AND OLIVE

220g cherry tomatoes, cut into 8

60g pitted green olives, quartered

3 tbsp extra virgin olive oil

2 garlic cloves, crushed

For the crab topping, gently mix the crab, Tabasco, chilli sauce, mayonnaise and 2 tsp of the chives in a large bowl.

Toast 4 slices of ciabatta on a griddle pan or in a toaster.

Divide the crab mixture into 4 and spoon it on the toasted ciabatta slices. Sprinkle over the remaining chives and serve.

For the mushroom bruschetta, pour the olive oil into a large frying pan and place over a medium heat. Add the garlic, rosemary and pancetta and fry for 5 minutes, stirring occasionally. Place in the mushrooms, chilli and ½ tsp salt, increase the heat and fry for 6 minutes, mixing well with a wooden spoon. Add the butter and Parmesan and cook for a further 2 minutes, allowing the butter to melt and create a slightly creamy texture.

Toast 4 slices of ciabatta on a griddle pan or in a toaster.

Divide the mushroom mixture into 4, spoon on top of the toasted ciabatta slices and serve.

To make the tomato topping, place the tomatoes, olives and extra virgin olive oil in a medium bowl, gently stirring to combine. Add the garlic and ¼ tsp salt, stir again, then allow to marinate for 15 minutes.

Toast 4 slices of ciabatta on a griddle pan or in a toaster.

Divide the tomato mixture into 4, spoon on top of the toasted ciabatta slices and serve.

RICOTTA AND SARDINIAN HONEY BRUSCHETTA

BRUSCHETTA CON RICOTTA E MIELE SARDO

◆◆◆◆◆◆◆◆◆◆◆◆◆◆◆◆◆◆◆◆◆◆◆◆◆◆◆◆

I have been lucky enough to travel throughout Italy over the years, experiencing wonderful ingredients and seeing how things such as cheeses are produced, but this year being able to make cheese with my family was definitely a highlight. Going to see Gianni Mele at his sheep farm in Lodè was fantastic, but actually herding and milking the sheep, then making fresh wonderful ricotta, was an incredible treat for all of us. This recipe is now a definite firm favourite of the D'Acampos. It's an epiphany of food for us: delicious, with every bite bringing back the memory of such a fantastic day.

SERVES 4–6

1 large loaf of bread, ciabatta or similar, cut into 1.5cm-thick slices

100ml extra virgin olive oil

2 garlic cloves, halved

350g ricotta cheese

finely grated zest of 1 unwaxed lemon

2 tbsp thyme leaves, plus more to serve, plus a couple of thyme flowers if you can find them

1 small red onion, very finely sliced

2 large, ripe tomatoes, roughly chopped

½ fennel bulb, finely sliced

2 tbsp local honey

fine sea salt and freshly ground black pepper

Preheat a griddle pan over a high heat. Rub each slice of bread with some of the olive oil on both sides to coat well, then toast on the griddle until golden and crunchy. When the bread is still hot off the griddle, rub each piece well with the whole garlic cloves so that the hot bread soaks in all the garlic flavour. (This is a great way to make garlic bread.)

Mix the ricotta in a medium bowl with the lemon zest, some more of the olive oil, the thyme leaves, salt and pepper.

Top each piece of the toasted garlic bread with a generous mound of ricotta. Then make a lovely bruschetta selection, topping a few with the sliced red onion, a few with the chopped tomatoes, and a few with slices of fennel, adding a few fennel fronds too, if you have them.

Drizzle each piece with more of the olive oil, season well with salt and pepper, add some more thyme and finally drizzle with the lovely local honey and garnish with the thyme flowers, if you found some. Serve immediately.

SUPER GREEN SOUP

ZUPPA DI VERDURE SUPER VERDE

◆◆◆◆◆◆◆◆◆◆◆◆◆◆◆◆◆◆◆◆◆◆◆◆◆◆◆

So many people ask me how to get more vegetables into their kids and my answer is always the same: keep getting them to try new things every time you make something! However, the truth is that the cheating parent's way is to hide the veg, and soup is the ultimate way to do that. This is a really tasty, healthy soup which takes just minutes to prepare and the whole family will love it. If you like your soup a little bit thicker, add a small peeled and chopped potato at the same time as the leeks.

SERVES 4

30g salted butter

1 medium leek, ends discarded, sliced into 1cm discs

1 large courgette, ends discarded, sliced into 1cm discs

250g broccoli florets

1.2 litres hot vegetable stock, made with stock cubes

100g spinach leaves, any coarse stalks removed

fine sea salt and freshly ground black pepper

Place the butter in a medium saucepan and set over a medium heat. Add the leek, courgette, broccoli, 1 tsp salt and ½ tsp pepper and fry for 6 minutes, stirring occasionally with a wooden spoon.

Pour in the hot stock, add the spinach and bring to the boil. Continue to cook for 20 minutes over a medium heat, then switch off the heat and let it rest for 5 minutes.

Using a hand-held blender, blitz until smooth.

Ladle into warmed bowls and serve with a twist of pepper and warm crusty bread.

GORGONZOLA, HONEY AND ASPARAGUS TARTLETS

TORTINI DI ASPARAGI, MIELE E GORGONZOLA

◆◆◆◆◆◆◆◆◆◆◆◆◆◆◆◆◆◆◆◆◆◆◆◆◆◆

Asparagus not only tastes great, but it's also incredibly good for you, full of nutrients including vitamins A, B6, C, E and K, as well as folate, iron, copper, calcium and protein. I love the look of this dish and the combination of flavours just work so well together, with the salty strong Gorgonzola and the sweetness of the honey. You can brush the borders of the tarts with chilli-infused olive oil instead of beaten egg if you prefer, which gives them a great kick. Once you are comfortable with the recipe, you can be as creative as you like with adding different cheese and vegetable toppings.

SERVES 4

200g fine asparagus spears, about 2cm of the woody ends removed

2 tbsp plain flour, to dust

320g ready-to-roll puff pastry

160g soft Gorgonzola cheese, at room temperature, smashed with a fork

1 egg, lightly beaten (or see recipe introduction)

4 tbsp honey

fine sea salt and freshly ground black pepper

Preheat the oven to 200°C/fan 180°C/Gas 6.

Pour 2.5 litres of water into a medium saucepan, add 1 tbsp salt, then bring to the boil and add the asparagus. Boil for 3 minutes, then drain and plunge into cold water, stopping the cooking process and ensuring the bright colour of the asparagus remains. Drain again and place on kitchen paper to allow any excess water to be absorbed. Season with salt and pepper and set aside.

Meanwhile, line a medium baking tray with baking parchment. Dust a clean work surface with flour and carefully roll out the puff pastry into a rectangle about 34 x 24cm. Cut into quarters and lay the pieces on the prepared baking sheet.

Gently spread one-quarter of the Gorgonzola on to each tart, leaving a 1cm border around the edges. Lay one-quarter of the asparagus evenly on top of the Gorgonzola on each tart and brush the pastry borders with beaten egg.

Bake for 15 minutes, or until the pastry has puffed up and is golden. Plate the tartlets and drizzle 1 tbsp honey over each, then serve immediately.

SALMON AND AVOCADO TARTARE WITH DILL AND BALSAMIC GLAZE

TARTARA DI SALMONE E AVOCADO CON ANETO E GLASSA DI ACETO BALSAMICO

◆◆◆◆◆◆◆◆◆◆◆◆◆◆◆◆◆◆◆◆◆◆◆◆◆◆◆

Living on the coast of Italy until I was eighteen, I was very privileged to always have fresh fish readily available. The fish were caught and sold on the same day, and, in my house, some seafood – for example razor clams – was often served raw with just a squeeze of lemon juice. My eldest son, Luciano, is a huge fan of avocados, so I combined my past and present and created this dish especially for him. Please try this, even if you are not a huge fish lover; it really is amazing and so easy, as well as insanely impressive at dinner parties.

SERVES 4

2 tbsp finely chopped dill, any coarse stalks removed

2 tbsp capers in brine, drained and roughly chopped

1 tbsp crème fraîche

1 tbsp Dijon mustard

1 lemon, plus lemon wedges to serve

2 small shallots, finely chopped

400g skinless salmon fillet

200g smoked salmon

2 large ripe avocados

4 tbsp balsamic glaze, plus a drizzle for decoration

8 slices of ciabatta, cut into 1cm-thick slices

4 tsp extra virgin olive oil

fine sea salt and freshly ground black pepper

Before you start, note that you can prepare the first 3 stages and place in the fridge separately, but do not mix until you are ready to serve, as the salmon will 'cook' in the lemon juice.

Stir the dill, capers, crème fraîche, mustard and 1 tbsp lemon juice together in a small bowl, cover and set in the fridge.

Place the shallots and the remaining lemon juice in another small bowl, mix, cover and set in the fridge.

Cut the salmon fillet and smoked salmon into small cubes, place in a medium bowl, mix, cover and set in the fridge.

When you are ready to serve, pour the crème fraîche and shallot mixes into the larger bowl of salmon and stir gently.

Peel and pit the avocados and chop into small cubes. Place in a medium bowl and add ½ tsp salt, ½ tsp pepper and the 4 tbsp of balsamic glaze. Stir gently.

Toast the bread on both sides, using a griddle pan or toaster.

Zig-zag balsamic glaze over 4 serving plates. Place a cooking ring in the centre of a plate. Spoon in one-quarter of the avocado and gently push down, covering the base evenly. Spoon one-quarter of the salmon on top, again pushing down. Gently lift off the ring. Repeat on all 4 plates.

Drizzle 1 tsp of extra virgin olive oil over each pile of salmon tartare and garnish each with a lemon wedge. Place 2 slices of toasted ciabatta on each plate and the dish is complete. Your guests will feel very spoilt.

MACARONI WITH FOUR CHEESES

MACCHERONI AI QUATTRO FORMAGGI

◆◆◆◆◆◆◆◆◆◆◆◆◆◆◆◆◆◆◆◆◆◆◆◆◆◆◆

I haven't met many people who don't love macaroni cheese. It's one of those dishes that you were given as a child, and eating it years later just makes you feel like you are being cuddled. All my family love this recipe. This dish has a new special place in my heart, as I will always think of Mia in Aggius learning a traditional Sardinian dance and how to weave a rug. You can add some English mustard to the sauce if you like a little kick, which works really well.

SERVES 4–6

500g dried pasta (pennette or penne, rigatoni, farfalle, pipe rigate, fusilli… whatever you like or have in)

250g mascarpone cheese

250g Gorgonzola cheese, crumbled

70ml whole milk

150g fresh peas, or frozen peas, defrosted

150g finely grated pecorino cheese, or Parmesan cheese

1 mozzarella ball, roughly chopped

fine sea salt and cracked black pepper

FOR THE PANGRATTATO

50ml olive oil

100g fresh white breadcrumbs

1 tsp paprika

First make the pangrattato by heating the olive oil in a frying pan before adding the breadcrumbs. Fry gently for 8–10 minutes in the oil until golden and crispy, then stir in the paprika and spoon on to kitchen paper to absorb excess oil.

Meanwhile, bring a large pan of salted water to the boil and cook the pasta.

Place a saucepan over a medium heat, add the mascarpone and stir to melt, then add the Gorgonzola. When the Gorgonzola has melted and the mix is bubbling gently, add the milk and some cracked black pepper, then tip in the peas and warm them through. Add half the pecorino, mix well, then turn off the heat.

When the pasta is cooked, use a slotted spoon to transfer the pasta directly to the sauce. Pop the heat back on, stir to make sure the pasta is well coated in the sauce, then add the chopped mozzarella and the rest of the pecorino. Keep stirring until the mozzarella has started to ooze and melt. Add in a handful of pangrattato and mix together before plating up. Top with the rest of the crunchy breadcrumbs and serve immediately.

PENNE WITH SMOKED PANCETTA AND MIXED WILD MUSHROOMS

PENNE CON PANCETTA AFFUMICATA E FUNGHI SELVATICI MISTI

Mushrooms can and should be cooked all year round, but, for me, eating mixed wild mushrooms in autumn takes me back home to Naples. The food markets there sold mushrooms mainly in October and November, and, at least once a week, we had some kind of pasta dish, or sauce, or bruschetta topping, made from various ingredients but always starring those mushrooms. This recipe was my sister Marcella's favourite and now has become a fixture at least once a month in our house.

SERVES 6–8

8 tbsp olive oil

3 garlic cloves, finely sliced

1 tbsp finely chopped
rosemary leaves

200g smoked pancetta,
finely chopped

600g mixed wild mushrooms, sliced

1 tsp chilli flakes

50g salted butter

80g finely grated Parmesan cheese

1kg dried penne pasta

fine sea salt

Pour 5 litres of water into a large saucepan, add 1½ tbsp salt and bring to the boil.

Meanwhile, pour the olive oil into a large shallow saucepan and place over a medium heat. Add the garlic, rosemary and pancetta and fry for 5 minutes, stirring occasionally. Place in the mushrooms, chilli and ½ tsp salt, increase the heat and fry for 10 minutes, mixing well with a wooden spoon. Add the butter and Parmesan and cook for a further 2 minutes, allowing the butter and cheese to melt into a creamy sauce. Switch off the heat under the mushrooms.

Cook the pasta until al dente (usually 1 minute less than instructed on the packet).

When the pasta is ready, drain, then return it to the large pan in which it was cooked. Reheat the mushroom sauce for 1 minute, then pour it into the large pan of cooked pasta. Stir well and serve: autumn in Naples, here we come!

LINGUINE WITH ANCHOVIES, GARLIC AND CHILLI

LINGUINA ALLA PUTTANESCA

◆◆◆◆◆◆◆◆◆◆◆◆◆◆◆◆◆◆◆◆◆◆◆◆◆◆◆◆

What a fantastic day this was. I was in Pisciotta, in Campania, with my in-laws, Elizabeth and Malcolm de Friend. We met a lovely man called Vittorio Rambaldo, who fishes anchovies, and his wife Donatella, who salts them. They have built up a strong family business which is now part of a Slow Food presidium, so I had to honour both them and the day by making a recipe with this amazing fish. I know people have a love/hate relationship with anchovies, but this recipe may even turn the haters!

SERVES 4

6 tbsp olive oil

2 garlic cloves, finely sliced

2 red chillies, finely sliced

30g salted capers, rinsed under cold water, then drained

50g pitted Taggiasche olives

8 anchovies in oil

2 x 400g cans of cherry tomatoes

handful of flat leaf parsley leaves, roughly chopped

500g dried linguine pasta

fine sea salt

Put the olive oil into a saucepan, then add the garlic. Turn the heat on to medium and allow the garlic to warm in the oil and become fragrant without burning. Add the chillies and fry for about 30 seconds, then add the drained capers. Switch off the heat to prevent the garlic from taking on any colour.

Add the olives and anchovies and turn the heat on once more, this time to low. Use a wooden spoon to break down the anchovies a bit before adding the tomatoes and the parsley. Leave to simmer while you cook the pasta.

Put the linguine into a large pan of salted boiling water and stir well. Cook until al dente (usually 1 minute less than instructed on the packet). When the pasta is ready, drain and place back into the pan with the sauce. Mix really well together and serve immediately.

FARFALLE WITH BROCCOLI, SALTED BUTTER AND CHEESE

FARFALLE CON BROCCOLI, BURRO E FORMAGGIO

◆◆◆◆◆◆◆◆◆◆◆◆◆◆◆◆◆◆◆◆◆◆◆◆◆

I came up with this recipe when my daughter Mia was a baby. She loved broccoli, so I threw some into already-boiling pasta water one day… and now we all love this dish! It is unbelievably quick, filling and full of flavour. You can substitute Cheddar cheese with any grated cheese of your choice, or, if you are a real cheese lover, use two different kinds; Parmesan works well.

SERVES 4

1 tbsp vegetable bouillon powder, or vegetable stock powder

500g dried farfalle pasta

350g broccoli, cut into florets

150g salted butter, at room temperature

100g grated Cheddar cheese, plus more (optional) to serve

fine sea salt and freshly ground black pepper

Pour 4 litres of water into a large saucepan, add the bouillon or stock powder and bring to the boil. Add the pasta and boil for 5 minutes, stirring occasionally. Place in the broccoli florets and boil for a further 6–7 minutes, depending on how al dente you like your pasta. (I cook mine for 1 minute less than instructed on the packet.)

Drain the broccoli and pasta in a colander. Place the butter in the hot saucepan and then pour back in the broccoli and pasta. Stir. Add the cheese and stir again, coating all the pasta with the butter and cheese.

Season with salt and pepper to taste and equally portion out the cheesy broccoli pasta between 4 warmed plates or bowls. Sprinkle over a little more cheese, if you like. Great for all the family and all done in less than 15 minutes.

CREAMY RISOTTO WITH COURGETTES, PEAS AND PEPPERS

RISOTTO CREMOSO CON ZUCCHINE, PISELLI E PEPERONI

We have risotto on the family menu at least once a week. I particularly love this quick version, and it gets lots of vegetables into the kids. My daughter Mia is not that keen on peppers, and yet, when they are in a creamy risotto, she never complains. This is a meal in itself, but I sometimes also top it with grilled balsamic chicken or some pan-fried garlic and chilli prawns. If, like me, you love adding a little kick to your meals, my tip is to either buy or make some chilli-infused olive oil and drizzle it over the top.

SERVES 4–6

8 tbsp olive oil

1 large red onion, finely chopped

1 tsp roughly chopped thyme leaves

1 large yellow pepper, deseeded and chopped into 1cm cubes

1 large courgette, chopped into 1cm cubes

500g arborio or carnaroli rice

150ml dry white wine

1.5 litres hot vegetable stock, made with stock cubes

200g frozen peas, defrosted

60g salted butter

60g finely grated Parmesan cheese

fine sea salt and freshly ground black pepper

Pour the oil into a large heavy-based saucepan, place over a medium heat and fry the onion, thyme, pepper and courgette for 10 minutes until soft, stirring with a wooden spoon.

Add the rice and fry for 3 minutes, stirring to allow the hot oil and vegetables to coat the grains. Stir in the wine and cook for a further minute, allowing the alcohol to evaporate.

Pour in a couple of ladles of hot stock and bring to a simmer. Reduce the heat and continue to cook and stir until all the stock is absorbed. At this point, please stay with the saucepan, because you need to keep stirring the risotto.

Stir in the peas. Pour in the rest of the stock, a little at a time, cooking until each addition is absorbed before you add the next. It will take 18–20 minutes and you may not need to add all the stock.

Once the rice is cooked, take the pan off the heat and add the butter, Parmesan, 2 tsp salt and ½ tsp pepper.

Stir all together for 20 seconds, allowing the risotto to become creamy and all the ingredients to combine properly. Serve on warmed plates and enjoy.

TAGLIATELLE WITH MIXED SEAFOOD, GARLIC AND WHITE WINE

TAGLIATELLE AI FRUTTI DI MARE CON AGLIO E VINO BIANCO

◆◆◆◆◆◆◆◆◆◆◆◆◆◆◆◆◆◆◆◆◆◆◆◆◆◆◆

If you ask me what my last supper would be, this would be it. I love most foods and have a very varied diet, but this recipe just takes me back in time, to when I was sitting round the kitchen table at my Nonna and Nonno's with my sister and a load of my cousins and tucking into this amazing meal. Living by the sea, we ate this at least once a week and I feel so lucky that I now get to share it with my own family. Make sure you have a small bowl of lemon water nearby: your hands will need it after!

SERVES 4

250g live mussels

250g live clams

100ml dry white wine

4 tbsp extra virgin olive oil

50g salted butter

4 garlic cloves, sliced

4 large langoustines

8 large unpeeled raw prawns

4 tbsp finely chopped flat leaf parsley leaves

350g dried tagliatelle pasta

20 cherry tomatoes, halved

finely grated zest of 1 unwaxed lemon, plus lemon wedges to serve

fine sea salt and freshly ground black pepper

Pour 4 litres of water into a large saucepan, add 1 tbsp salt and bring to the boil.

Scrub the mussels and clams under cold running water. Rinse away the grit and remove any barnacles with a small, sharp knife. Remove the 'beards' from the mussels by pulling the dark, stringy pieces away from the shells. Drop the clams from a height into a large bowl a few times, to help them expel their sand, then wash briefly in cold water for a couple of minutes. Check none of the clams are open or broken, and, if they are, discard them. Discard any open mussels or clams that do not shut when tapped firmly on the sink, or any which have broken shells.

Place the mussels and clams in a medium saucepan, pour in the wine and cook with the lid on over a medium heat for 5 minutes. Tip into a colander set over a bowl, so you can save the juices, discard any that remain closed and set aside.

Put the olive oil and butter into a large frying pan and melt the butter over a medium heat. Add the garlic and gently fry until it begins to sizzle. Pour in the cooking juices from the mussels and clams – leaving behind the very last of the juices which might contain grit – and simmer for 2 minutes. Season with ¾ tsp salt and ½ tsp pepper and stir occasionally.

Now stir in the langoustines and prawns and fry them for 1½ minutes. Using tongs, turn them over and continue to

cook for a further 1½ minutes until they all turn pink all over. Add the mussels and clams with the parsley and stir until heated through, about 2 minutes.

Meanwhile, cook the pasta in the boiling water until al dente; my preference is to cook it for 1 minute less than instructed on the packet, giving the perfect al dente bite. Drain and tip back into the large saucepan you cooked it in. Pour over the seafood sauce, add the tomatoes and lemon zest and toss all together over a low heat for 30 seconds, allowing the flavours to coat the pasta.

Remove the prawns and langoustines and place on a plate, (this will make it easier to serve up the pasta, mussels and clams). Equally divide the pasta between 4 warmed serving plates or bowls, then top each portion with a langoustine and 2 prawns. Serve with lemon wedges. For me, this is my favourite meal of all time.

pictured overleaf

RIGATONI WITH CHIPOLATAS, COURGETTES AND MASCARPONE

RIGATONI CON SALSICCE, ZUCCHINE E MASCARPONE

◆◆◆◆◆◆◆◆◆◆◆◆◆◆◆◆◆◆◆◆◆◆◆◆◆◆◆◆◆◆

I actually created this recipe as an argument-stopper. My daughter Mia wanted pasta and my boys really fancied a meatier meal. I had some chipolata sausages left over and so this dish came about by me basically throwing what I had in the fridge together to please them all. It is now one of our family favourites! You can use any sausages you like (obviously increase the cooking time a little if they are much bigger), and substitute the Parmesan cheese with pecorino, if you prefer. Peas instead of courgettes also work well.

SERVES 4

6 tbsp olive oil

1 large onion, finely chopped

500g chipolata sausages, chopped into 2cm pieces

1 large courgette, chopped into 5mm cubes

200g pancetta, diced

500g dried rigatoni pasta

250g mascarpone cheese

100ml milk, at room temperature

60g finely grated Parmesan cheese, plus more (optional) to serve

fine sea salt and freshly ground black pepper

Pour 4 litres of water into a large saucepan, add 1 tbsp salt and bring to the boil.

Meanwhile, pour the olive oil into a large shallow saucepan and place over a medium heat. Add the onion and fry for 8 minutes. Place in the chopped sausages, courgette and pancetta and fry for 20 minutes, stirring occasionally with a wooden spoon.

After about 15 minutes of cooking the vegetables and sausages, put the pasta into the boiling water and cook for 1 minute less than instructed on the packet, giving you the perfect al dente bite.

Spoon the mascarpone into the sausage mix and add a ladle of the boiling water from your cooking pasta. Add the milk to the sausage sauce and stir well until combined. Sprinkle in the Parmesan, 1 tsp salt and ½ tsp pepper and allow to simmer for 2 minutes, stirring continuously. Turn off the heat and set aside.

When the pasta is ready, drain, then return it to the large pan in which it was cooked. Pour over the chipolata sauce and stir well, ensuring all the pasta is coated in the sauce. Equally divide the pasta between 4 warmed plates or large bowls and enjoy, sprinkled with a bit more cheese, if you like.

TUNA PATTIES WITH LEMON ZEST AND SPRING ONIONS

POLPETTE DI TONNO CON SCORZA DI LIMONE

◆◆◆◆◆◆◆◆◆◆◆◆◆◆◆◆◆◆◆◆◆◆◆◆◆◆◆

This recipe is amazing, considering you can make it and eat it within ten minutes. I have suggested putting the patties into the fridge before frying, to help them stay together in the pan, but, to be honest, I have also fried them straight after making them, and, if you are gentle, they work fine. You can substitute the spring onions for shallots, onions or chives if you prefer. Perfect for a light brunch or lunch.

SERVES 4 AS A STARTER, OR 2 AS A LIGHT LUNCH

5 cans of tuna in oil, drained (400g drained weight in total)

25g fine breadcrumbs

1 tsp English mustard

1 tbsp lemon juice

1 tsp finely grated unwaxed lemon zest

1 tbsp chopped spring onions (about 4)

½ tsp Tabasco sauce

1 large egg, lightly beaten

1 tbsp extra virgin olive oil

15g salted butter

fine sea salt and freshly ground black pepper

Place the drained tuna, breadcrumbs, mustard, lemon juice and zest, spring onions and Tabasco sauce in a large bowl. Mix well, then taste and season with salt and pepper. Now add the egg, and, using your hands, combine together.

Divide the tuna mixture into 8 equal balls, rolling gently in your hands, then flatten each into a patty. Place them on some greaseproof paper or baking parchment on a plate or tray and put into the fridge for 1 hour, if you have time. Otherwise just cook them now.

Heat the olive oil and butter in a large frying pan over a medium heat. Gently place the tuna patties in the pan and cook for 3 minutes (you may need to do this in batches). Turn them over using a spatula and continue to cook for another 3 minutes. Remove and place on some kitchen paper to allow any excess oil to drain away.

Serve with your favourite salad.

PAN-FRIED SEA BASS FILLETS IN LEMON AND CAPER SAUCE

FILETTI DI SPIGOLA AL LIMONE E CAPPERI

◆◆◆◆◆◆◆◆◆◆◆◆◆◆◆◆◆◆◆◆◆◆◆◆◆◆◆◆

I originally created this sauce to go with chicken: the sharpness of the lemon with the salty capers is such a great combination that works with most white fish or white meat and keeps everything beautiful and moist. Feel free to substitute the sea bass for haddock or cod fillets, chicken breasts or veal escalopes. It is so quick and easy to prepare, really versatile and tastes fantastic.

SERVES 4

40g plain flour, to dust

4 sea bass fillets with skin on, about 250g each

4 tbsp olive oil

80g salted butter

juice of 2 lemons

2 tbsp small capers in brine, drained

50ml white wine

4 tbsp finely chopped flat leaf parsley leaves

fine sea salt and freshly ground black pepper

Put the flour on to a large plate, season with ½ tsp salt and ½ tsp pepper and mix. Coat both sides of the sea bass fillets with the flour. Gently tap the fish to discard any excess flour and set aside.

Place a large frying pan over a medium heat, pour in the olive oil and add half the butter. Once the butter has melted, place the sea bass fillets into the pan skin-side down and fry for 3 minutes. Turn the fillets over carefully using a spatula and fry for a further minute until cooked through. Remove the fillets and keep warm on a large serving plate covered with foil while you make the sauce.

Pour the lemon juice, capers and wine into the same frying pan, and, with the help of a wooden spoon, scrape all the brown bits from the edges and base of the pan into the sauce. Bring to the boil and stir for 1 minute.

Add the parsley and remaining butter and continue to stir for a further minute until you create a creamy texture.

To serve, place a sea bass fillet on each of 4 warmed serving plates and drizzle over the lemon and caper sauce. Serve immediately, with new potatoes, roast asparagus or any salad of your choice.

CHICKEN GOUJON WRAPS
WITH TRUFFLE MAYONNAISE

INVOLTINI DI POLLO CON MAIONESE AL TARTUFO

✦✦✦✦✦✦✦✦✦✦✦✦✦✦✦✦✦✦✦✦✦✦✦✦✦

A firm favourite for a quick lunch or dinner, as everyone can make their own wraps. I have included all the ingredients I love, but you can use any grated cheese and my family all prefer different sauces. Mia has plain mayonnaise, Rocco has sweet chilli sauce and Jessica has sour cream and chive. Luciano also loves to add bacon and salad to his. I simply fry the chicken and plate up all the other ingredients, then everyone digs in and builds their own wraps. If you are being healthy, grill the chicken with no breadcrumbs instead and add lettuce and light Caesar dressing. This recipe is how to keep everyone happy, made easy!

SERVES 4

2 eggs

16 mini chicken fillets, about 750g in total

100g fine breadcrumbs, toasted

200ml vegetable oil

8 tortilla wraps

16 tsp truffle mayonnaise

2 large avocados, peeled, pitted and smashed with a fork

8 tbsp grated Cheddar cheese

fine sea salt and freshly ground black pepper

Crack the eggs into a large bowl and lightly beat with a fork. Add the chicken fillets, making sure you coat all the pieces. Set aside.

Place the breadcrumbs on a medium flat tray and season with ½ tsp salt and ½ tsp pepper. Dip each chicken fillet into the seasoned breadcrumbs, pressing down slightly, then flip the pieces over and coat the other side.

In the meantime, pour the oil into a shallow saucepan and place over a high heat. When the oil is hot (you can test this by adding a small pinch of breadcrumbs; they should sizzle), place in half the chicken. Fry for 4 minutes, then turn the fillets over and fry for a further 4 minutes. Take out and place on a large plate lined with kitchen paper, allowing the excess oil to drain off, then sprinkle over a pinch of salt. Fry the remaining chicken in the same way.

When ready, take a warmed-through tortilla wrap (follow the instructions on the packet to warm them, usually about 35 seconds in a microwave), and spread over 2 tsp truffle mayonnaise. Spoon over one-quarter of an avocado (about 1 tbsp), sprinkle over 1 tbsp of cheese and arrange 2 chicken goujons on top. Roll into a sausage shape. Repeat the process, giving each person 2 wraps, or just put everything in the middle of the table and let everyone build their own, using as much of everything as they prefer.

RIBEYE STEAK WITH CREAMY SPINACH AND MARSALA

BISTECCA CON SPINACI CREMOSI AL MARSALA

◆◆◆◆◆◆◆◆◆◆◆◆◆◆◆◆◆◆◆◆◆◆◆◆◆◆◆

For me, there is nothing better than a good-quality steak. Ribeye is my preferred choice, but you can use any cut that you like for this recipe. Many of you, my wife included, like to have some kind of sauce drizzled over the top, so I came up with this recipe as a perfect compromise. I get to eat a simply cooked steak, but the beautiful creamy spinach underneath it means that everyone's happy. The most important tip I can give you is not to season your steak with salt before or during cooking, or you will dry out the meat.

SERVES 4

4 ribeye steaks, each about 300g

250g spinach leaves, any coarse stalks removed

50ml Marsala wine

300ml double cream

¼ tsp nutmeg, ideally freshly grated

3 tbsp olive oil

2 rosemary sprigs

knob of salted butter

fine sea salt and freshly ground black pepper

sea salt flakes

Take the steaks out of the fridge and bring them to room temperature before you start cooking.

Place a medium frying pan over a high heat and pile in half the spinach. Cook for 1 minute, then add the remaining leaves. Sprinkle over a large pinch of fine salt and mix well with tongs. Cook for 2 minutes, or until all the leaves have wilted.

Tip the spinach into a sieve over a sink, and, pushing down with your tongs, release and discard any excess water. Place the spinach on a chopping board, and, with a large knife, roughly chop it. Return the spinach to the frying pan and set over a high heat. Pour in the Marsala and (carefully) tip the pan away from you towards the flame to ignite the alcohol, enabling it to evaporate. Cook for 30 seconds, then pour in the cream, mix all together, reduce the heat to medium and let it cook for 5 minutes, stirring occasionally with a wooden spoon. Add the nutmeg, ½ tsp fine salt and ½ tsp pepper, stir and cook for a further 5 minutes. Set aside.

Meanwhile, put the steaks on a large flat plate and pour over 2 tbsp of the olive oil. Sprinkle over 2 pinches of pepper and gently rub the peppery oil all over both sides of the steaks.

Set a large non-stick frying pan over a high heat for 2 minutes, allowing the pan to get really hot. Place the steaks in the pan and cook for 3 minutes. Do not touch or move the steaks around: the more you touch them, the more moisture can be released and the tougher they will get.

Turn the steaks over and cook for a further 3 minutes, to give medium-rare steaks. (Cook for an extra minute on each side if you prefer your meat slightly more cooked.) Take the pan off the heat and add the rosemary, butter and the remaining 1 tbsp of oil. Move and turn the steaks around, ensuring both sides of the meat are coated. Return to the heat and continue to fry for a further minute, using a tablespoon to baste the top of the steaks with the flavoured juices from the pan.

Remove the steaks from the pan and place on a chopping board, cover with foil to keep warm and rest for 5 minutes.

Meanwhile, warm up the creamy spinach over a low heat for 5 minutes, stirring with a wooden spoon occasionally.

Cut all the steaks into 6–7 diagonal slices each and sprinkle a pinch of sea salt flakes over each steak.

Equally divide the creamy spinach between 4 warmed serving plates. With the help of a tablespoon, create a slight hollow in the centre of each spinach bed. Place the steak slices on top and serve immediately.

pictured overleaf

ONE POT

I don't know about you guys, but, for me, there is nothing better than throwing some well-chosen ingredients into a single container – a pan, a baking tray, or even sealed inside a sheet of foil – and just letting the magic happen. All the recipes in this chapter make use of good ingredients and great seasoning… and then it is up to the oven or hob to do its job with very little effort from you at all. These are my one pot wonders!

Some of the dishes here you will only need to come back to when they're done, leaving you time to focus on the kids or just relax, while others need a little bit more attention, but all of them are really easy to prepare.

I think my absolute favourite in this chapter is the 'sausage in the hole' (obviously), and I also love the lamb casserole and the grilled salmon. My eldest son Luciano isn't that keen on salmon, so we often use the same marinade from that recipe on cod or sea bass fillets, as we all love its sweet balsamic flavour.

As suggested in some of the recipes, you can substitute the main ingredient as long as you stick to the same method. They are very versatile. For example, the spicy pork rib recipe can become a chicken or even a cod dish and it will still be fantastic. Although there is only one risotto in this chapter – as you do have to stay by the pot for the entire time during cooking – it is very worthwhile and so simple to do. (It's also great for kids, as it has protein, veg and carbs all in the same pot.) Each version of risotto gives you a completely different-flavoured meal, so do try some of the other risottos in this book if you're looking for other delicious one pot dishes.

This way of cooking is perfect for all occasions and it was quite hard to narrow the chapter down to just eighteen recipes! I have tried to give you some great dishes here that can also be adaptable to fit in with your lives and everyone's likes and dislikes. I hope you love them and that they make your family dinner time that little bit easier.

◆◆◆◆◆◆◆◆◆◆◆◆◆◆◆◆◆◆◆◆◆◆◆◆◆◆◆◆

MARINATED SALMON WITH MAPLE SYRUP, GARLIC AND BALSAMIC VINEGAR

SALMONE MARINATO CON SCIROPPO D'ACERO, AGLIO E ACETO BALSAMICO

◆◆◆◆◆◆◆◆◆◆◆◆◆◆◆◆◆◆◆◆◆◆◆◆◆◆◆◆◆◆◆

I love salmon, it is such a healthy oily fish that cooks very quickly. You can grill it simply with just a touch of olive oil, salt and pepper, or add soy sauce and ginger to this recipe for a completely different flavour; it never disappoints. (If you're going for the soy sauce option, substitute the parsley here for chives and don't add any salt.) This is also great cooked on the barbecue.

SERVES 4

3 tbsp extra virgin olive oil

1 garlic clove, crushed

4 tbsp balsamic vinegar

3 tbsp maple syrup

3 tbsp finely chopped flat leaf parsley leaves

4 skinless salmon fillets, about 160g each

4 sprigs of cherry tomatoes on the vine, about 110g per sprig

fine sea salt and freshly ground black pepper

Pour the extra virgin olive oil into a medium bowl, add the garlic, balsamic vinegar and maple syrup and whisk all together. Stir in the parsley with 1 tsp salt and 1 tsp pepper.

Place the salmon in the bowl with the marinade, making sure that all the surfaces of the fish are coated. Cover with cling film and leave to marinate, at room temperature, for 15 minutes. After 10 minutes, please move the salmon around, to make sure the fish is marinated all over.

Preheat the grill to high.

Line a baking tray with foil. Gently remove the salmon from the marinade using tongs and place the fillets on the prepared tray, leaving large spaces between each.

Carefully dip a sprig of cherry tomatoes into the marinade and place next to a salmon fillet. Repeat this process for the other tomato sprigs, again placing each next to a fish fillet.

Cook under the grill for 3 minutes, then turn the fish and tomatoes over and continue to grill for a further 3 minutes. Please do not overcook the salmon, or it will become dry.

Serve with boiled new potatoes dressed with a little extra virgin olive oil, salt and pepper.

ROASTED COD PARCELS WITH CAPERS, OLIVES AND WHITE WINE

MERLUZZO AL CARTOCCIO CON CAPPERI, OLIVE E VINO BIANCO

◆◆◆◆◆◆◆◆◆◆◆◆◆◆◆◆◆◆◆◆◆◆◆◆◆

This has to be one of the easiest recipes in the book. You literally put everything into some foil, wrap it up and cook for twenty-two minutes. It looks great, tastes great, is incredibly good for you and takes minutes to prepare. You can top the fish with red or green pesto instead if you prefer, which also works fantastically. I often serve this with roasted asparagus and boiled new potatoes, but any seasonal vegetable will complement it.

SERVES 4

2 large beef tomatoes

4 skinless, boneless chunky cod loin portions, about 160g each

4 tsp capers in brine, drained

16 pitted black olives

4 tbsp finely chopped flat leaf parsley leaves

1 lemon, quartered

4 tbsp white wine

8 small tsp salted butter

fine sea salt and freshly ground black pepper

Preheat the oven to 200°C/fan 180°C/Gas 6.

Slice the tomatoes into 5mm-thick slices; you need 8 good slices, so just eat the rest.

Place a large sheet of foil on a clean work surface. Take 2 slices of tomato and put them in the centre of the foil. Gently place 1 portion of cod loin on top. Pile 1 tsp capers, 4 olives and 1 tbsp of parsley on top of the fish. Squeeze over a lemon quarter and sprinkle over a large pinch each of salt and pepper.

Fold up the sides of the foil, leaving the top open. Pour over 1 tbsp wine and finally place 2 small tsp of butter on top of the fish (1 tsp on each end). Pinch the foil together, so it makes a parcel, sealing the fish inside completely. Place on a medium baking tray.

Repeat the process to make and seal all 4 cod parcels.

Place on a baking sheet in the middle of the oven and roast for 22 minutes.

When ready, put each cod parcel on a warmed plate and carefully open up the foil (there will be hot steam released). I love to serve it in the parcel, as it looks rustic and allows the sauce to be contained. Serve with your favourite seasonal vegetables, rice or boiled potatoes.

WHOLE ROASTED SEA BREAM WITH ASPARAGUS AND GREEN BEANS

ORATA AL FORNO CON ASPARAGI E FAGIOLINI

Many of my friends tell me they won't even try recipes like this, as they find it a little annoying to serve the fish, but trust me, once you have learned how to do it, it gets easier and easier, I promise. It is such a quick simple way to cook fish; the bones keep it moist and it looks amazing when you bring it out to serve. I particularly like this recipe, as I've combined some favourite Chinese flavours with traditional Italian ingredients and it works fantastically.

SERVES 4

1.2kg whole sea bream, gutted, cleaned and scaled with head, tail and skin on

7 tbsp extra virgin olive oil

500g asparagus spears, about 2cm of the woody ends removed

400g fine green beans

2 rosemary sprigs

2 garlic cloves, peeled

3 thin slices of fresh root ginger

1 unwaxed lime

fine sea salt and freshly ground black pepper

FOR THE DRESSING

5 tbsp extra virgin olive oil

1 tsp finely grated fresh root ginger

3 tbsp soy sauce

3 spring onions, finely sliced

juice of ½ lime

Preheat the oven to 200°C/fan 180°C/Gas 6.

Wash the fish well under cold tap water. Drizzle 5 tbsp of the oil on a large oven tray. Add the asparagus, beans, 1 tsp salt and ½ tsp pepper, and, using your hands, mix well, ensuring the vegetables are well coated in the oil. Push the vegetables to the sides of the tray, creating a space for the fish to lie diagonally. Place the sea bream in the space and drizzle and rub over the remaining 2 tbsp of oil. Place the rosemary sprigs, garlic and ginger in the belly cavity of the fish. Cut 2 x 1cm-thick slices of lime and stuff into the fish belly. Roast in the oven for 40 minutes.

Meanwhile, prepare the dressing. Pour the oil into a small bowl with 2 tbsp cold water and add the ginger, soy sauce, spring onions and lime juice. Whisk all together for about 40 seconds to create a dressing.

When the fish is cooked, equally divide the vegetables between 4 warmed plates. Remove the skin from the sea bream and divide the fish between the plates. Drizzle the dressing over the fish and serve immediately.

ROASTED VEGETABLES AND GOAT'S CHEESE

VERDURE AL FORNO CON FORMAGGIO DI CAPRA

We absolutely love this recipe in my house. The flavour combinations work perfectly, with the sweet balsamic glaze, strong goat's cheese and wonderful vegetables. In the past, I have added roasted butternut squash and toasted pine nuts, which also makes a lovely meal, but I think this is my favourite version. It is also a really great-looking dish to serve if you are having guests over.

SERVES 4 AS A STARTER, OR 2 AS A MAIN COURSE

2 courgettes, cut into 1cm half-moons

1 large onion, cut into 1cm slices

2 large red onions, cut into 1cm slices

4 peppers (2 yellow, 1 orange, 1 red), deseeded and cut into 2cm slices

5 tbsp olive oil, plus more for brushing the ciabatta

1 ciabatta loaf

1 garlic clove, halved

200g goat's cheese

balsamic glaze, to taste

fine sea salt and freshly ground black pepper

Preheat the oven to 220°C/fan 200°C/Gas 7.

Place the courgettes, onions, peppers, the 5 tbsp of olive oil, 2 tsp salt and 1 tsp pepper in a large oven tray, and, using your hands, mix together. Roast in the oven for 1 hour, stirring every 20 minutes.

About 10 minutes before the vegetables are due to be ready, put a large griddle pan over a high heat for 5 minutes. Cut the ciabatta into 8 diagonal slices, each 2cm thick. Brush with a little oil on both sides, then place on the griddle pan and toast for 2 minutes on each side. Transfer to a plate. Gently rub one side of the toast with the garlic clove and set aside.

If this is your main meal, then spoon the vegetables on 2 large warmed plates and place 100g of goat's cheese in the centre of each. Drizzle over some balsamic glaze and serve each with 4 ciabatta slices.

If this is a starter, spoon one-quarter of the vegetables on to 4 small warmed plates, place 50g of goat's cheese in the centre of each and drizzle over some balsamic glaze. Serve each with 2 ciabatta slices.

PASTA WITH SLOW-COOKED CAULIFLOWER, PANCETTA AND PARMESAN

PASTA CAVOLFIORI COTTI LENTAMENTE CON PANCETTA E PARMIGIANO

◆◆◆◆◆◆◆◆◆◆◆◆◆◆◆◆◆◆◆◆◆◆◆◆

This is such an amazing one pot recipe and a huge D'Acampo family favourite that I just had to put it in this book. It is the perfect autumn and winter dish and we have had it for lunch or dinner over and again; it is so comforting, filling, super-easy to make and absolutely delicious. You can substitute the Parmesan for pecorino cheese, or use *mezzi* rigatoni (short rigatoni pasta shapes) instead of conchiglie, if you prefer.

SERVES 4

1 large cauliflower, about 1kg

1 large onion, finely chopped

7 tbsp olive oil

200g pancetta, diced

1 vegetable stock cube

1 tbsp tomato purée

500g dried conchiglie pasta
   (medium shells)

60g finely grated Parmesan cheese

60g salted butter

fine sea salt and freshly ground
   black pepper

Remove the cauliflower leaves. Sit the cauliflower on a work surface and cut it in half through the stalk. Cut away the core centre stalks from both halves (discard them, or use in soup): the florets will separate. Cut each floret in half and set aside.

Place a large saucepan over a high heat and add the onion and oil. Fry for 8 minutes, stirring occasionally with a wooden spoon. Add the pancetta and fry for a further 6 minutes, again stirring occasionally. Set a full kettle of water on to boil.

Add the cauliflower to the pancetta and stir for 2 minutes, scraping the pan to release the caramelised flavours.

Pour in 1 litre of boiling water from the kettle and again scrape the bottom of the saucepan using a wooden spoon for about 2 minutes. Fill and boil the kettle once more. Crumble the stock cube into the pan, add 1 tsp salt, or to taste, and pour in a further 2 litres of boiling water from the kettle. Stir all together, reduce the heat to a minimum, half-cover with a lid and simmer for 1 hour, stirring occasionally.

Stir in the tomato purée and another 1 tsp salt, or to taste, and pour in a further 300ml of boiling water from the kettle. Stir and leave to simmer gently for 40 minutes. Add the pasta and cook in the simmering broth for about 16 minutes (taste the pasta to check it has an al dente bite), stirring occasionally with a wooden spoon.

Switch off the heat and gently stir in the Parmesan, butter and 1 tsp pepper. Keep stirring for about 30 seconds until the butter has melted. Let it rest for 5 minutes and then serve; this is so worth the cooking time!

CHICKEN IN WHITE WINE WITH CARROTS AND ROSEMARY

POLLO COTTO IN VINO BIANCO CON CAROTE E ROSMARINO

How can this recipe not be delicious when it is cooked in a whole bottle of wine? You can already taste the flavour in your mouth just by reading the ingredients list. This can be served as is, with some warm bread and seasonal greens of your choice, or we love it with plain boiled rice, so the gravy has something else to flavour. It is perfect with roast asparagus on the side, too. This is a firm favourite for us.

SERVES 4

1 large onion, finely chopped

1 tbsp finely chopped rosemary leaves

4 tbsp olive oil

2 large carrots, cut into 1cm cubes

8 bone-in, skin-on chicken thighs, about 1.4kg in total

1 bottle of white wine

½ tsp vegetable bouillon powder, or vegetable stock powder

fine sea salt and freshly ground black pepper

Put the onion, rosemary, olive oil and carrots into a shallow saucepan. Season with 1 tsp salt and fry over a high heat for 10 minutes.

Move the vegetables to one side of the pan and place half the chicken on the other side, skin-side down, so the skin is in contact with the pan. Move the veg on top of the chicken, then place in the remaining thighs, skin-side down, into the empty side of the pan, again so the skin touches the base. Fry for 8 minutes. Turn the chicken, again making sure it touches the pan base, and fry for a further 2 minutes.

Pour the wine over the chicken. Add the bouillon or stock powder and ½ tsp pepper, bring to the boil, then reduce the heat to medium and simmer for 10 minutes, uncovered.

Turn the chicken over and cook for a further 10 minutes. Then turn the chicken for the last time and cook for a final 15 minutes.

To serve, place 2 chicken thighs on each of 4 warmed plates, remove the skin if you want, and, using a slotted spoon, divide the vegetables over the chicken.

CHICKEN RISOTTO WITH BALSAMIC GLAZE

RISOTTO CON POLLO E GLASSA DI ACETO BALSAMICO

◆◆◆◆◆◆◆◆◆◆◆◆◆◆◆◆◆◆◆◆◆◆◆◆◆◆

My son Rocco loves balsamic glaze, so once, when making a chicken risotto, I drizzled some over his dish. It tasted lovely, so I decided to incorporate it into a risotto recipe. Although this is a one pot wonder, you do need to make sure that you are constantly stirring, so please only make this recipe if you have the time to stand and stir for twenty-five or thirty minutes. I promise, it will be worth it. You can substitute the chicken with sausagemeat if you prefer, or the Parmesan with Grana Padano cheese.

SERVES 4

8 tbsp olive oil

1 large onion, finely chopped

1 courgette, finely chopped

3 large skinless chicken breast fillets (about 550g in total), cut into 3cm chunks

3 tbsp balsamic glaze, plus more to serve

500g arborio or carnaroli rice

200ml white wine

1.5 litres hot chicken stock

150g frozen peas, defrosted

60g salted butter

60g finely grated Parmesan cheese

fine sea salt and freshly ground black pepper

Heat the olive oil in a large saucepan over a medium heat and add the onion and courgette. Fry for 15 minutes until the onion has softened. Add the chicken and balsamic glaze and stir with a wooden spoon. Cook for 4 minutes, stirring occasionally. Pour in the rice and coat it in the flavours for 3 minutes, stirring every minute. Pour in the wine, stir and let simmer for 2 minutes.

Spoon in 3 ladles of the hot stock and simmer for 4 minutes, stirring continuously until the liquid has been absorbed. Pour in the rest of the stock, a little at the time, cooking until each addition is absorbed before you add the next. It will take about 18 minutes and you may not need to add all the stock. Once the rice is cooked (it should have an al dente bite), stir in the peas.

Remove the saucepan from the heat and stir in the butter, Parmesan, 1 tsp salt and ½ tsp pepper. Stir for about 30 seconds until creamy. To serve, spoon the risotto on to warmed plates and drizzle over some more balsamic glaze. Finally, you can put that wooden spoon down and enjoy!

SAUSAGE IN THE HOLE

PASTICCIO DI SALSICCE

◆◆◆◆◆◆◆◆◆◆◆◆◆◆◆◆◆◆◆◆◆◆◆◆◆◆◆◆

If any of you watch *This Morning* on ITV, you will know why I have called this recipe 'sausage in the hole' rather than toad in the hole; you must agree that toad in the hole doesn't sound as appetising… I have created individual ones, as I feel it looks nicer served this way, and also the crispy Yorkshire pudding doesn't become as soggy. Sometimes we all get a bit fancy when catering for guests, but wouldn't it be amazing to be served this recipe with onion gravy, mash and peas? I know I would be ecstatic. If you are vegetarian, just substitute the chipolatas for Quorn sausages. You will need two four-hole Yorkshire pudding trays with large moulds.

SERVES 4

100g plain flour

3 large eggs

150ml milk (whatever you have in the fridge is fine)

16 pork chipolatas

8 tsp sunflower oil

fine sea salt and freshly ground black pepper

Place the flour, eggs, milk, 1 tsp salt and ½ tsp pepper in a medium jug and whisk until all the ingredients are combined. Leave in the fridge for 1 hour.

Preheat the oven to 220°C/fan 200°C/Gas 7.

Cut all the sausages in half widthways and place 2 sausages (4 halves) in each hole of the tins. Cook in the oven for 15 minutes. Now, using oven gloves, as the tins will still be hot, pour 1 tsp sunflower oil into each Yorkshire mould and rotate them around slightly, allowing the oil to cover the bottom and sides. Return to the oven for 5 minutes.

Turn the sausages over so they are browned-sides down and pour the batter on top, dividing it equally between the tins. Put back into the oven for a further 15–18 minutes, or until the batter has risen well and is browned.

Serve 2 sausages in the hole to each person on warmed plates with mash, peas and onion gravy, or, if you prefer, just some green seasonal vegetables.

SAUSAGE AND BEAN STEW WITH ROSEMARY AND CHILLI

SALSICCE E FAGIOLI CON ROSMARINO E PEPERONCINO

◆◆◆◆◆◆◆◆◆◆◆◆◆◆◆◆◆◆◆◆◆◆◆◆◆

Every time we come to Sardinia during the colder months, we always have a trip to the beach to make this dish. There is something so special about cooking simply outside and everyone just digging into the pan with forks. Any pork sausages will work, but the fatty ones do give an extra flavour. Outside eating doesn't just have to be for summer: if you buy a portable hob ring, this can be made literally anywhere and just tastes so much better outdoors, somehow.

SERVES 4–6

6 tbsp olive oil, plus more
  for brushing

1 tbsp roughly chopped
  rosemary leaves

½ tsp chilli flakes

2 medium red onions, finely sliced

900g Italian sausages, or other
  good-quality pork sausages

2 x 400g cans of borlotti beans

2 x 400g cans of cannellini beans

400ml hot vegetable stock, made
  with stock cubes

1 tablespoon tomato purée

3 tbsp chopped flat leaf parsley leaves

1 ciabatta loaf

1 large garlic clove, halved

fine sea salt

Place a large saucepan over a high heat and pour in the oil with the rosemary, chilli, onions and 1 tsp salt. Stir all together and fry for 12 minutes, stirring occasionally.

Meanwhile, place the sausages on a chopping board and cut into 4cm pieces. Set aside.

Open the cans of beans and drain off any excess juices, but please do not drain the beans completely as a little of their juices will help to create a smooth, thick sauce.

Put the sausages into the saucepan with the onions and fry for 10 minutes, stirring every 2 minutes to allow them to seal all over in the oil. Add the beans with the hot stock and the tomato purée. Stir all together and bring to the boil.

Reduce the heat to medium and cook for 20 minutes, uncovered, stirring every 3–4 minutes. Once it's ready, switch off the heat, stir in the parsley and let it rest for 10 minutes.

Meanwhile, preheat a griddle pan over a high heat. Slice the bread diagonally about 2cm thick. Brush a little olive oil on both sides and griddle for 1 minute on each side. Gently rub the garlic clove on both sides of the bread.

Serve the sausages and beans in warmed serving plates or bowls with your home-made ciabatta garlic bread.

PORK RIBS IN A SPICY TOMATO SAUCE

COSTOLETTE DI MAIALE IN SALSA DI POMODORO PICCANTE

◆◆◆◆◆◆◆◆◆◆◆◆◆◆◆◆◆◆◆◆◆◆◆◆◆◆◆◆◆

Barbecued ribs are definitely a winner in the D'Acampo house, but, of course, standing over a barbecue in winter rain is not much fun. So here is a way to cook ribs with far less effort, spending most of the cooking time sitting on the sofa! If you are a fan of tomato sauces, this recipe is definitely for you. You can add pitted black olives if you wish. The sauce is also amazing with chicken thighs or cod fillets, but the cooking time for those would be less.

SERVES 4

3 x 400g cans of plum tomatoes

1 tsp dried oregano

3 tsp chilli flakes

1 large onion, finely chopped

2 medium carrots, cut into small chunks

1 vegetable stock cube

4 tbsp olive oil

2 tbsp runny honey

16 medium-sized pork ribs, about 1.5kg in total (make sure they are very meaty)

fine sea salt

Preheat the oven to 200°C/fan 180°C/Gas 6.

Empty the cans of plum tomatoes into a large bowl. Fill 1 can with water and pour this into the bowl, too. Add 2½ tsp salt, the oregano, chilli, onion and carrots and crumble over the stock cube. Pour in the olive oil and honey.

Using your hand, gently squeeze the plum tomatoes between your fingers and combine all the ingredients together.

Place the ribs in a large oven tray and pour over the spicy tomato mixture, ensuring the meat is well covered by the sauce. Cover with foil and cook in the middle of the preheated oven for 1 hour.

Take out the tray, remove and discard the foil and stir. Reduce the oven temperature to 190°C/fan 170°C/Gas 5 and then return the ribs to the oven for 30 minutes. Take the oven tray out again, turn the ribs over and put back into the oven for a final 30 minutes.

Serve with warm crusty bread – so you can dunky-dunky the sauce – and a fresh salad or corn on the cob on the side would make it perfect.

ITALIAN LAMB CASSEROLE WITH SHALLOTS, POTATOES AND MINT SAUCE

STUFATO DI AGNELLO CON SCALOGNO, PATATE E SALSA ALLA MENTA

I know I am a huge advocate for eating seasonal ingredients, but there are some exceptions to the rule and this recipe is definitely one of them. In the UK, lamb is ready to eat from spring to early autumn, but because in this recipe we are cooking it in the oven for a long time, this casserole can definitely be eaten all year round, as the meat will always become tender and delicious. It really is one of the tastiest yet easiest recipes to make in this book, and we eat it at least once a month in my house.

SERVES 4

2 tbsp white wine vinegar

4 tbsp finely chopped rosemary leaves

1 tbsp good-quality mint sauce

4 tbsp runny honey

800g neck of lamb fillet, fat trimmed off, cut into 3cm cubes

10 shallots, peeled

3 large carrots, cut into 2cm chunks

2 large potatoes, each cut into 8

400ml red wine

300ml vegetable stock, made with stock cubes

3 tsp cornflour

fine sea salt and freshly ground black pepper

In a large bowl, mix the vinegar, rosemary, mint sauce, honey, 1 tsp salt and ½ tsp pepper. Add the lamb and stir well, making sure the meat is well coated. Cover with cling film and place in the fridge for about 4 hours.

Preheat the oven to 190°C/fan 170°C/Gas 5.

Place the shallots, carrots and potatoes in a small casserole dish and stir with a wooden spoon. Add the marinated lamb with its juices, the wine and stock. Mix well, put the lid on top and place in the middle of the preheated oven for 1 hour.

Take out the casserole dish, stir, then put back into the oven for 40 minutes, still with the lid on.

Put the cornflour into an espresso cup, add 5 tbsp of cold water and stir to combine. Take out the lamb casserole and add the cornflour mixture. Stir the meat and gravy and put back into the oven, this time without the lid on, for a final 30 minutes.

Remove from the oven and allow to rest for 15 minutes. Serve with some fluffy rice or warm crusty bread.

SUPER-TASTY MEATLOAF WITH PARMA HAM AND BOILED EGGS

POLPETTONE SUPER DELIZIOSO CON PROSCIUTTO CRUDO E UOVA SODE

◆◆◆◆◆◆◆◆◆◆◆◆◆◆◆◆◆◆◆◆◆◆◆◆◆◆◆◆◆

As many of you know, my daughter Mia loves meatballs, so much so that there is another recipe in this book called Mia's Meatballs (see page 168), but she asked for them so much that, as a family, we were getting a little bit bored with them, so I came up with this recipe as an alternative. Using almost the same ingredients, but cooking them together in the oven, gives you a completely different meal. You can substitute the Parma ham with any ham of your choice if you prefer, and please serve it with my amazing Brussels Sprouts and Chorizo (see page 88) for the perfect combination.

SERVES 6

2 tbsp olive oil

5 slices of white or brown bread, crusts discarded

200ml milk (whatever you have in the fridge is fine)

500g minced pork

500g minced beef

2 tbsp finely chopped flat leaf parsley leaves

1 large garlic clove, crushed

70g finely grated Parmesan cheese

1 egg

9 slices of Parma ham

5 large hard-boiled eggs

fine sea salt and freshly ground black pepper

Take a medium baking tray with a rim and cover it with baking parchment. Pour over 1 tbsp olive oil and spread it out to cover the baking tray. Set aside.

Break the bread up into a large bowl and pour over the milk. Using your fingertips, mix the bread and milk together to create a wet paste. Add the minced meats and combine together. Now add the parsley, garlic, Parmesan, 2 tsp salt and ½ tsp pepper and crack in the egg. At this point, use your hand to mix all the ingredients together.

Take half the meat mixture and roll it in your hands, creating an oval ball. Place this in the middle of the prepared baking tray and gently flatten it out to create an oval shape about 25 x 15cm and 1cm thick. Place 3 Parma ham slices on top, covering the meat.

Cut 5mm off each end of the eggs and place them end-to-end down the centre of the ham-covered meatloaf, leaving a gap at each end of about 2cm. Place 1 slice of Parma ham on top of the eggs, then put 1 slice on each long side of the line of eggs. Place another slice again on top of the eggs and 1 more slice on each short side, so all the Parma ham slices have now been used and the eggs are encompassed completely.

Take the remaining meat mixture and again roll in your hands creating an oval ball, then flatten it to about the size of the meatloaf. Gently place it on top of the eggs and pat down the sides, enclosing the ham and eggs. Seal by pinching the 2 halves of the meatloaf together. Pour the remaining 1 tbsp olive oil into your hands and smooth it over the meat. Using the back of a spoon, smooth out any cracks in the meat and ensure that the sides are sealed all around. Cover the meatloaf with cling film and refrigerate for 30 minutes.

Remove the cling film, and, using your hands, lightly squeeze the top and sides of the meatloaf again, to make sure it is compact. Leave to rest at room temperature for 15 minutes. Meanwhile, preheat the oven to 200°C/fan 180°C/Gas 6.

Completely cover the meatloaf with foil, tucking it under the baking tray rim; this will keep the meatloaf moist. Roast in the oven for 30 minutes. Remove the foil and continue to cook for a further 40 minutes. Take the meatloaf out of the oven and leave to rest for 5 minutes. Slice and serve with my amazing Brussels Sprouts and Chorizo.

pictured overleaf

BRUSSELS SPROUTS AND CHORIZO

CAVOLETTI DI BRUXELLES E CHORIZO

◆◆◆◆◆◆◆◆◆◆◆◆◆◆◆◆◆◆◆◆◆◆◆◆◆◆◆◆◆

Sprouts are like Marmite – you either love them or hate them – but I'm a true believer that the haters have probably only tried plain boiled sprouts. So I urge those people to please give this recipe a try and then decide. All my family love sprouts cooked this way, and, as a side dish, it can go with almost anything, from grilled fish to most roast meats. This dish is always on the table when we are serving up my Super-Tasty Meatloaf with Parma Ham and Boiled Eggs (see page 84), so do please make them together.

SERVES 4 AS A SIDE DISH

4 tbsp olive oil

1 large onion, finely chopped

½ tsp chilli flakes

150g chorizo, finely chopped

500g Brussels sprouts, trimmed, then par-boiled for 5 minutes

3 tbsp maple syrup

fine sea salt

Pour the olive oil into a shallow saucepan and set over a high heat. Add the onion and chilli and fry for 3 minutes, stirring occasionally with a wooden spoon. Add the chorizo and continue to fry for a further 8 minutes, stirring occasionally.

Pour in the par-boiled and well-drained Brussels sprouts, then add the maple syrup and a pinch of salt. Reduce the heat to medium and fry for 4 minutes, stirring occasionally. So quick and easy, but the flavours together are amazing.

pictured on page 87

SIMPLE SPICY SPINACH WITH GARLIC AND OLIVE OIL

SPINACI AGLIO, OLIO E PEPERONCINO

◆◆◆◆◆◆◆◆◆◆◆◆◆◆◆◆◆◆◆◆◆◆◆◆◆◆

This had to go into my one pot wonder chapter, as not only is it incredibly good for you, but it is also very versatile. I have put this spinach in omelettes, on toasted bread as a bruschetta topping (extra-special crowned with a poached egg), or, of course, served it as a simple accompaniment to almost any meal. It will literally take you twelve minutes from start to finish and is completely delicious. Don't be fooled by the large quantity of spinach: it wilts right down.

SERVES 4 AS A SIDE DISH

5 tbsp olive oil

3 garlic cloves, finely sliced

½ tsp chilli flakes

500g spinach leaves, any coarse
  stalks removed

fine sea salt

Place the oil, garlic and chilli in a large saucepan and set over a high heat for about 1 minute. As soon as the garlic starts to sizzle, add half the spinach. Reduce the heat to medium and cook for 2 minutes, stirring occasionally with tongs (this allows you to pick up leaves and move them around easily).

The cooked spinach should be wilted enough to now add the rest of the leaves. Cook for a further 2 minutes, again using the tongs to move the leaves around and ensuring the spinach on top is cooked too. Add 1 tsp salt and continue to stir and cook for another 2 minutes.

Increase the heat to high and fry for 5 minutes, allowing the excess water to evaporate. Serve with anything!

pictured on page 205

FESTIVE SIDES

CONTORNI PER LE FESTIVITÀ

◆◆◆◆◆◆◆◆◆◆◆◆◆◆◆◆◆◆◆◆◆◆◆◆◆◆◆

Side dishes are hugely important in Italy. They have just as much attention given to them, often more so, as the main meal. My wife would argue that my roast potatoes are the star of the show when they are served with any meal, while my home-made apple sauce, which I created to go with our roast pork at Christmas, is also great with my Apple and Pork Burgers with Garlic and Oregano (see page 120). All of the side dishes here should definitely be given a go and not only on festive occasions!

GINO'S ROAST POTATOES

SERVES 4–6

700g new potatoes, halved or quartered where necessary so they are all the same size

3 large peppers (1 yellow, 1 red, 1 green), deseeded and sliced

6 garlic cloves, whole, bashed

6 tbsp olive oil

2 tbsp roughly chopped rosemary leaves

fine sea salt and freshly ground black pepper

Preheat the oven to 220°C/fan 200°C/Gas 7.

Mix the potatoes, peppers, garlic, olive oil and rosemary with 1 tsp salt and plenty of pepper in a large roasting dish.

Toss well and roast for 20 minutes. Remove from the oven, turn the potatoes and roast for a further 20 minutes until golden and tender. Serve with any main dish of your choice.

pictured overleaf

SPICY BRUSSELS SPROUTS

SERVES 4–6

500g Brussels sprouts

4 tbsp olive oil

1 large onion, finely chopped

1 tsp chilli flakes

3 tbsp honey

fine sea salt

Par-boil the Brussels sprouts for 5 minutes in a saucepan of boiling water, then drain well.

Pour the olive oil into a shallow saucepan and set over a high heat. Add the onion, chilli and a pinch of salt and fry for 4–5 minutes, stirring occasionally.

Pour in the drained sprouts and add the honey with another pinch of salt. Reduce the heat to medium and fry for a final 4–5 minutes, or until the sprouts have caramelised slightly. Serve immediately.

pictured overleaf

APPLE SAUCE

SERVES 4–6

3 large cooking apples, peeled, cored and finely sliced

juice of ½ lemon

Place a pan over a medium heat and add the apples, lemon juice and 200ml of water. Bring to a simmer, then reduce the heat and leave to cook for 10–15 minutes, stirring occasionally, until the apples are completely soft but haven't taken on any colour.

When the apples are soft, transfer to a blender and blitz well. Pass through a sieve to make it extra smooth, if you like, and serve immediately.

pictured overleaf

ITALIAN ROASTED RIB OF BEEF

COSTATA DI MANZO ARROSTO

◆◆◆◆◆◆◆◆◆◆◆◆◆◆◆◆◆◆◆◆◆◆◆◆◆

We never really had this kind of meat growing up; my family preferred chicken thighs or roasted pork or lamb and I'm sure it was because a really good rib of beef in the south of Italy – or anywhere actually – is quite expensive. I am lucky now to be able to make this recipe quite often for my family and I know it may sound silly but that really makes me feel good, not only because I am serving up a truly fantastic-tasting dish, but also because I am treating them to something really special which, in my childhood, I never really had. I hope you and your family enjoy this recipe as much as we do.

SERVES 6

2.8kg rib of beef

2 large onions

2 large carrots, halved widthways, then halved lengthways

4 rosemary sprigs

1 tbsp olive oil

200ml red wine

sea salt flakes and freshly ground black pepper

Take the rib of beef out of the fridge 1 hour before cooking, allowing it to come to room temperature. Preheat the oven to 210°C/fan 190°C/Gas 6½.

Cut 5mm off each end of the onions and discard. Cut each onion into 4 discs (leaving the skin on, as we are using them as a stand and for flavour, not for eating) and lay them in a roasting tray. Place the carrots on top, creating a rack-like effect. Put the rosemary sprigs on top of the carrots.

In a small bowl, pour in the oil, add 1 tbsp sea salt flakes and ¼ tbsp pepper and stir to combine. Pat the meat dry using kitchen paper, and, with a sharp knife, score the fat, but not the meat. Pour over the oil marinade and rub it all over the beef. Gently place the meat on top of the vegetable rack and put it on a low shelf in your oven to roast for 20 minutes.

Reduce the oven temperature to 180°C/fan 160°C/Gas 4 and roast for 40 minutes. Remove from the oven, pour the wine over the vegetables (not over the beef as you want this to be crusty), and return to the oven for 40 minutes. Increase the oven temperature to 200°C/fan 180°C/Gas 6, and, for medium-rare beef, cook for a final 15 minutes. (If you prefer your beef medium, then cook for a final 25 minutes.)

Take out of the oven and leave to rest for 10 minutes before slicing and serving. This is amazing with crushed potatoes and seasonal vegetables.

LIGHTER

◆◆◆◆◆◆◆◆◆◆◆◆◆◆◆◆◆◆◆◆◆◆◆◆◆◆◆◆

Italians love to eat a lot of courses. Getting friends and family over for a big meal, sitting round the table all afternoon or into the evening is just the perfect way to spend your time – there's nothing like it – and we are all, obviously, huge foodies in the D'Acampo household. I do think that food and life are all about balance, though, which is where the recipes in this chapter come in. They are for when we feel we need to be a little bit careful with what we eat, or healthier, as I prefer to say! I decided to create some lighter recipes that we can enjoy all year round, that are easy to prepare and super-tasty.

This is definitely not a diet chapter, so please do not look at this section and think that eating these dishes means you will be missing out on delicious food, or even sacrificing anything at all. The recipes here are a regular part of our family menu and we honestly do not even notice any difference. There are pasta recipes, a luxurious cheesy risotto, roast chicken, and even lobster for a special occasion. All the recipes can be served to the entire family and many of them are perfect for dinner parties. I have just been a little bit mindful with either the portion size or the ingredients, making sure each meal comes in at around five hundred calories (or fewer, in most cases). By cutting back on the butter or oil or sugar, these lower-calorie crowd-pleasers can be freely enjoyed…

I think if you stay active and eat well then there shouldn't be a need to diet, but I also know that when family life is full-on, sometimes eating well can fall to the bottom of the list, so I hope these recipes will help!

◆◆◆◆◆◆◆◆◆◆◆◆◆◆◆◆◆◆◆◆◆◆◆◆◆◆◆◆

LUCIANO'S FAVOURITE BREAKFAST

LA COLAZIONE PREFERITA DI LUCIANO

◆◆◆◆◆◆◆◆◆◆◆◆◆◆◆◆◆◆◆◆◆◆◆◆◆◆

This recipe is dedicated to my son Luciano. He absolutely loves eggs and could eat them every day for breakfast, brunch or lunch. He would hoover up a double portion of this, but a single serving is more than enough and will provide all the good fats and protein you need. You can substitute the Parma ham for plain cooked lean ham if you prefer.

SERVES 4

1 tsp white wine vinegar

2 avocados, peeled and pitted

4 slices of wholemeal bread

4 slices of Parma ham

4 large eggs

fine sea salt and freshly ground
   black pepper

Place 700ml water into a small saucepan and bring to the boil over a medium heat. Add the white wine vinegar.

In the meantime, using a fork, smash the avocados in a bowl, add 1 tsp salt and ½ tsp pepper and mix well.

Toast the bread.

Lay a slice of Parma ham on each slice of toast and equally divide the seasoned avocado on top. Set aside.

Crack 2 eggs on the side of the saucepan and gently open them into the boiling water. You can crack them into a small bowl or cup and then lower them in gently, if you prefer. Let them simmer in the water for 2 minutes for a runny egg. Using a slotted spoon, gently pick up an egg and hold it above the water to drain slightly. Place 1 egg on each prepared toast, season with salt and pepper and serve immediately, as the egg will continue to cook if not broken.

Repeat the process for the other eggs. I prefer to poach just 2 at a time, making sure I get the cooking time right and each egg perfect.

MINESTRONE

ZUPPA DI VERDURE

✦✦✦✦✦✦✦✦✦✦✦✦✦✦✦✦✦✦✦✦✦✦✦✦✦✦✦

You will look at this ingredients list and wonder how some of them can possibly be allowed in a lower-calorie section. It just goes to show that, cooked in the right way, no foods are off limits. This has to be one of my favourite soups of all time and it will keep you filled up for hours. If you decide to make this recipe in the morning for later in the day, cook it up to the point when you are about to put in the pasta. Only add the pasta and cook for the last twenty-five minutes when you are ready to serve, or the pasta will go soggy.

SERVES 6

3 tbsp olive oil

2 onions, finely chopped

2 carrots, finely chopped

2 celery sticks, finely chopped

200g canned cannellini beans, drained

250g King Edward potatoes, chopped into 2cm chunks

200g dark green cabbage (cavolo nero), any coarse stems removed, leaves roughly chopped

400g can of chopped tomatoes

200g French beans, finely chopped

2 litres vegetable stock, made with stock cubes

120g dried conchigliette pasta (baby shells)

4 tbsp roughly chopped flat leaf parsley leaves

fine sea salt and freshly ground black pepper

60g finely grated pecorino cheese, to serve

Heat the olive oil in a large saucepan over a medium heat and fry the onions, carrots and celery for 10 minutes, or until they are just golden.

Add the cannellini beans, potatoes, cabbage, chopped tomatoes, French beans and stock and bring to the boil.

Reduce the heat, half-cover the saucepan with the lid and cook for 30 minutes, stirring occasionally.

Remove the lid, add the pasta with the parsley and continue to cook over a medium heat for a further 25 minutes, stirring occasionally. Season to taste (I like to add ½ tsp pepper).

Check that all the vegetables are tender and the pasta is cooked and serve immediately in warmed bowls, with a sprinkle of pecorino cheese on top.

SMOOTH TOMATO SOUP
WITH CARAMELISED RED ONIONS

CREMA DI POMODORO CON CIPOLLE ROSSE CARAMELLIZZATE

◆◆◆◆◆◆◆◆◆◆◆◆◆◆◆◆◆◆◆◆◆◆◆◆◆◆◆

If you're looking for a recipe that is healthy, tasty and super-quick to make, then this soup ticks all the boxes. No need for fancy or expensive ingredients and all done, ready to serve, in thirty minutes. If you want to make a bigger batch, the recipe is easy to scale up, so you can also portion it up and either take it with you to the office, where it will last in the fridge for up to three days, or freeze it in portion-sized servings.

SERVES 4

1 large or 2 small red onions, sliced

2 medium carrots, chopped into small cubes

2 tsp sugar

4 tbsp extra virgin olive oil

2 x 400g cans of chopped or plum tomatoes

6–8 basil leaves

fine sea salt and freshly ground black pepper

Place the onion(s) and carrots into a medium saucepan and sprinkle over the sugar, 1 tsp salt and ¼ tsp pepper. Pour over the oil and place over a medium heat. Cook for 10 minutes, stirring occasionally with a wooden spoon.

Pour over 400ml of boiling water and cook for 10 minutes, stirring occasionally.

Tip in the tomatoes with the basil and continue to cook for a further 10 minutes, stirring occasionally.

Use an electric hand-held blender to blitz the soup until smooth. Serve in warmed soup bowls.

Buon appetito!

SPICY BEAN SOUP WITH CELERY AND PANCETTA

ZUPPA DI FAGIOLI PICCANTE CON SEDANO E PANCETTA

My family often has odd splurges of healthy eating, but we can get very bored with salads, especially during the autumn and winter months. This recipe is perfect for those occasions. It is so filling and rich in flavour, not to mention incredibly good for you. You can leave out the pancetta if you prefer a vegetarian option, and it tastes just as good if you prefer to use pecorino cheese instead of Parmesan. I have created this to be quite spicy, so decrease the amount of chilli if you're serving it to younger children.

SERVES 6

4 tbsp olive oil

200g pancetta, diced

3 garlic cloves, crushed

1 tbsp thyme leaves

2 carrots, finely chopped

1 celery stick, finely chopped

3 tsp chilli flakes

400g can of cannellini beans, drained

400g can of chickpeas, drained

400g can of green lentils, drained

400g can of borlotti beans, drained

1 litre vegetable stock, made with stock cubes

fine sea salt and freshly ground black pepper

60g finely grated Parmesan cheese, to serve

In a medium saucepan, heat the olive oil over a high heat and fry the pancetta, garlic, thyme, carrots, celery and chilli for 10 minutes, or until golden.

Add in all the beans and pulses, pour in the stock and bring to the boil. Season with salt and pepper to taste.

Reduce the heat, half-cover the saucepan with a lid and cook for 30 minutes, stirring occasionally with a wooden spoon. Take off the heat and allow to rest for 10 minutes.

Once ready, serve into warmed soup bowls and sprinkle over the Parmesan cheese. Perfection in a bowl!

SUPER-QUICK TUNA AND BEAN SALAD

INSALATA VELOCISSIMA CON TONNO E FAGIOLI

◆◆◆◆◆◆◆◆◆◆◆◆◆◆◆◆◆◆◆◆◆◆◆◆◆◆

This recipe reminds me of our family summer holidays in Sardinia. We often eat it for lunch, especially if we are having a beach or boat day out, because it can be prepared in the morning and boxed up for later, giving you the perfect packed lunch. The flavours are so fresh and the beans and tuna will leave you very full. If you are having a dinner party and preparing fish as your main course, this also makes a great starter.

SERVES 4

400g can of chickpeas, drained

400g can of red kidney beans, drained

400g can of butter beans, drained

1 red onion, finely sliced

1 lemon

2 tbsp extra virgin olive oil

1 tbsp chopped chives

10 cherry tomatoes, halved

1 tbsp balsamic glaze

4 thin slices of crusty bread

1 garlic clove, halved

400g can of tuna in oil, drained

fine sea salt and freshly ground
    black pepper

Place all the pulses and beans in a large bowl with the sliced onion. Squeeze in the juice of half the lemon and pour in the olive oil. Mix well.

Add the chives, tomatoes and balsamic glaze and season with salt and pepper. Mix all together and leave to rest for 10 minutes at room temperature.

Meanwhile, toast the bread on both sides on a griddle pan or in a toaster and rub one side of the toast with the garlic. Place each slice in the middle of a serving plate.

Gently fold the tuna into the bean salad and serve on top of the prepared garlic bread. So tasty and filling.

CREAMY RISOTTO WITH ASPARAGUS, PEAS AND GORGONZOLA

RISOTTO CREMOSO CON ASPARAGI, PISELLI E GORGONZOLA

Over the years I have made so many different risotto combinations, but this one is dedicated to my son Luciano. He absolutely loves cheeses, the smellier and bluer the better. My go-to for making a risotto creamy is always Parmesan cheese and butter, but, actually, using a creamy blue cheese means you end up needing far less (or none) of those and it still gives a really strong, rich flavour. You can substitute the Gorgonzola with any other soft blue cheese of your choice, if you prefer.

SERVES 4

200g fine asparagus spears, about 2cm of the woody ends removed

150g frozen peas, defrosted

3 tbsp olive oil

1 medium onion, finely chopped

250g arborio or carnaroli rice

150ml white wine

900ml hot vegetable stock, made with stock cubes

1 tsp salted butter, at room temperature

60g Gorgonzola cheese, at room temperature, crumbled

fine sea salt and freshly ground black pepper

Cut each asparagus spear into 6 pieces on the diagonal and place in a small bowl with the peas. Set aside.

Pour the olive oil into a medium heavy-based saucepan, place over a medium heat and fry the onion for 10 minutes until soft, stirring with a wooden spoon. Add the rice and ½ tsp pepper and continue to fry for 3 minutes, stirring continuously with a wooden spoon and allowing the hot oil to coat the rice grains completely.

Stir in the wine and cook for a further minute, allowing the alcohol to evaporate. Pour in a couple of ladles of stock and bring to a simmer. Reduce the heat and continue to cook, stirring occasionally, until all the stock is absorbed.

At this point, please stay with the saucepan, because you need to keep stirring with a wooden spoon. Add the asparagus and peas and combine.

Pour in the rest of the stock, a little at the time, cooking until each addition is absorbed before you add the next. It will take about 18 minutes and you may not need to add all the stock. Once the rice is cooked (it should have an al dente bite), take it off the heat, add the butter and Gorgonzola and stir all together for 20 seconds, allowing the risotto to become creamy and all the ingredients to combine properly. Season with salt to taste and serve on 4 warmed plates.

LARGE PASTA SHELLS WITH PEPPERS, AUBERGINES AND PECORINO CHEESE

CONCHIGLIONI CON VERDURE E PECORINO

◆◆◆◆◆◆◆◆◆◆◆◆◆◆◆◆◆◆◆◆◆◆◆◆◆

When I first made this recipe for my children, I really thought I would get some kickback, as quite often Rocco and Mia tell me they are not keen on aubergines or peppers. We have a rule at home that you have to try everything put in front of you and this recipe goes to show that philosophy really works. Both kids ate the lot and loved it; Rocco even wanted seconds! I personally love mine with a bit of kick, so, if you are the same, substitute the olive oil for chilli-infused oil. If you can't find huge pasta shells for this, you can of course use regular-sized shells, although you may want to up the quantity.

SERVES 4

4 tbsp extra virgin olive oil

1 large onion, finely chopped

1 small aubergine, cut into 1cm cubes

1 large red pepper, deseeded and cut into 1cm cubes

2 large courgettes, about 600g in total, cut into 1cm cubes

100g cherry tomatoes, halved

300g dried conchiglioni pasta (extra-large shells), or 500g dried conchiglie pasta (medium shells)

10 basil leaves

30g finely grated pecorino cheese

fine sea salt and freshly ground black pepper

Fill a large saucepan with 4 litres of water, add 1 tbsp salt and bring to the boil over a high heat.

Meanwhile, pour the olive oil into a large frying pan and place over a medium heat. Fry the onion for 3 minutes until softened. Add the aubergine and cook for 8 minutes, then add the pepper and continue to fry for 6 minutes, stirring occasionally. Add the courgettes, tomatoes, 1 tsp salt and ½ tsp pepper, mix well and cook for a further 8 minutes. Keep stirring occasionally.

Cook the pasta in the boiling water until al dente. To get the perfect al dente bite, cook the pasta for 1 minute less then instructed on the packet and always cook it with the lid off. Stir every minute or so.

Once the pasta is cooked, drain well and tip it back into the same saucepan, off the heat. Pour over the vegetables, add the basil and cheese and mix all together for 20 seconds, allowing all the flavours of the vegetables to coat the pasta.

Serve immediately on warmed plates.

PAPPARDELLE WITH SPICY BEEF AND WILD MUSHROOMS

PAPPARDELLE PICCANTI CON MANZO E FUNGHI SELVATICI

I came up with this recipe when I had some leftover beef fillet in the fridge, and we usually have mushrooms in, so I just threw these brilliant ingredients together. We all loved it and it became a firm favourite at home. The kids prefer the large flat ribbons of pappardelle, but of course you can substitute tagliatelle or linguine if you prefer. It is so rich and delicious that you won't believe it comes in at less than five hundred calories for each portion.

SERVES 4

240g lean fillet steak, cut into 2cm cubes

1 tbsp plain flour

2 tbsp extra virgin olive oil

1 tsp chilli flakes

200g mixed wild mushrooms, roughly sliced

100ml red wine

1 tbsp tomato purée

200ml beef stock

350g fresh egg pappardelle pasta

fine sea salt

Pour 4 litres of water into a large saucepan, add 1 tbsp salt and bring to the boil.

Place the steak in a large bowl and dust the pieces with the flour, turning to coat all sides. Pour the olive oil into a medium frying pan and gently fry the beef over a medium heat for 3 minutes, turning, until browned all over. Remove the meat with a slotted spoon, place on a plate and set aside.

Add the chilli flakes and wild mushrooms to the pan and fry for 5 minutes, stirring occasionally. Pour in the wine and bring to the boil. Return the beef to the pan, add the tomato purée and gently stir. Pour in the stock and stir again. Return to the boil, then reduce the heat to low, cover with a lid and cook for 30 minutes.

Remove the lid and cook for a final 5 minutes, allowing the sauce to thicken slightly. Season with salt to taste.

Cook the fresh pasta as instructed on the packet; fresh pasta usually only needs 4–5 minutes. Stir with tongs to ensure the ribbons have separated, drain, then return it to the saucepan.

Pour over the chilli beef and mushroom sauce and stir well, ensuring the pasta is well coated. Divide between 4 warmed plates or large bowls and enjoy.

GRILLED LOBSTERS WITH LEMON AND EXTRA VIRGIN OLIVE OIL

ARAGOSTA ALLA GRIGLIA CON OLIO E LIMONE

◆◆◆◆◆◆◆◆◆◆◆◆◆◆◆◆◆◆◆◆◆◆◆◆

I know that this is quite an extravagant meal, but to treat yourself – especially when you are calorie-watching – seems only fair. I absolutely love lobsters and always grill them on a barbecue if I can, giving them that extra-smoky flavour. For a bit of a kick, adding some chilli flakes or a little mustard to the dressing is also lovely.

SERVES 4

5 fish stock cubes

4 large lobsters (about 600g each), very fresh

6 tbsp extra virgin olive oil

1 tsp cayenne pepper

3 garlic cloves, crushed

15g flat leaf parsley leaves, finely chopped

juice of 2 lemons

fine sea salt and freshly ground black pepper

Put 8 litres of water into a very large saucepan with the fish stock cubes and bring to the boil.

Place the lobsters in the boiling water for 5 minutes, then, using tongs, take them out and immediately place them in a sink of iced water for a further 5 minutes. Finally, drain the lobsters, head down, in a colander for 10 minutes. Remove the claws and crack them, cut the bodies in half lengthways and set aside.

Preheat a griddle pan over a high heat, or a barbecue to its hottest setting.

In the meantime, pour the olive oil into a small bowl. Add the cayenne pepper, garlic, parsley, lemon juice, 1 tsp salt and ½ tsp pepper and mix well. Brush the marinade all over the lobster meat and set aside.

Place the lobsters, meat-side down, on the griddle pan or barbecue and cook for 2 minutes. Turn them over and cook shell-side down for 5 minutes. The meat should be firm and opaque all the way through. Serve with a tomato and avocado salad, or – if you are hungry and not watching calories, and while the pan or barbecue is hot – turn your meal into a surf and turf and throw on some lovely ribeye steaks.

ROAST CHICKEN WITH ROSEMARY AND LEMON

POLLO ARROSTO CON ROSMARINO E LIMONE

◆◆◆◆◆◆◆◆◆◆◆◆◆◆◆◆◆◆◆◆◆◆◆◆◆

There are so many different recipes you can make with chicken, as it is such a versatile meat that most people love. The greatest thing about a traditional roast chicken is that you can put it into the oven and go about your way until it's ready. The trick is to keep it moist and this recipe does just that, while also serving up a delicious gravy, so there's another job less to do. My secret ingredient of strawberry jam is the equivalent of cranberry sauce with turkey: a match made in heaven. (It is actually a good addition to most meat gravies.) Just in case your chicken is bigger or smaller than the bird I cooked here, remember you need to cook it for twenty minutes for every 500g, and then add an extra twenty-five minutes at the end.

SERVES 4

1 large onion, finely sliced

2kg whole chicken

1 lemon, halved

3 rosemary sprigs

2 tsp chicken seasoning spice

4 tbsp olive oil

1 tsp strawberry jam

1 tsp English mustard

1½ tbsp honey

fine sea salt and freshly ground black pepper

Preheat the oven to 200°C/fan 180°C/Gas 6.

Place the sliced onion in a large roasting tin. Fill the chicken with the lemon halves and 1 rosemary sprig and put it on top. Sprinkle over the chicken spice, 1 tsp salt and ½ tsp pepper and place the other rosemary sprigs on each leg of the bird. Pour the olive oil over the chicken and onion and place in the oven for 1 hour 20 minutes.

Remove from the oven and place the chicken on a plate. Add the strawberry jam, mustard, ½ tsp of the honey and 125ml of boiling water to the roasting tin with the onion, (some of which will be singed, but we are using it all here). Stir well, creating a gravy, and season to taste.

Return the chicken to the roasting tin and spoon over some of the gravy juices. Pour the remaining honey over the chicken and return it to the oven for a final 25 minutes.

When ready, plate up your chicken; I'm personally a leg and thigh man. Pour the delicious gravy into a jug and serve with seasonal vegetables.

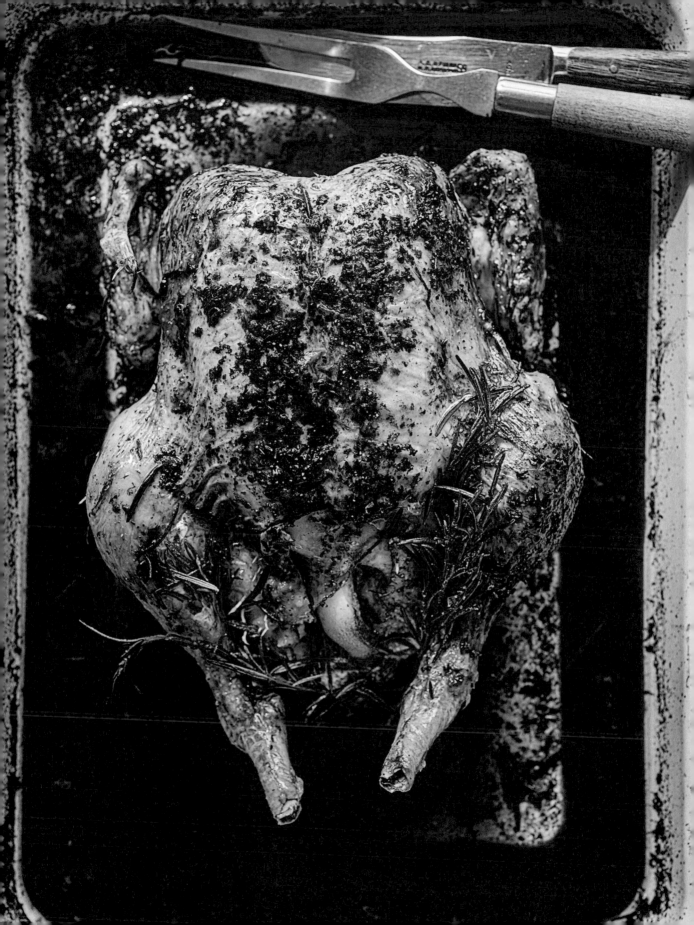

APPLE AND PORK BURGERS WITH GARLIC AND OREGANO

HAMBURGER DI MAIALE E MELE CON AGLIO E ORIGANO

I love the flavours of these burgers. The apple and pork are perfect together. Here, I have used dried oregano, although sage also works well, and – of course – you can brush each burger with the olive oil and cook on a hot griddle pan or barbecue instead, if you prefer that to frying. This recipe always gets a thumbs-up, so I hope you like it as much as we do.

SERVES 4

500g minced pork, 5 per cent fat or less

30g fresh breadcrumbs

2 garlic cloves, crushed

1 tsp dried oregano

1 medium apple, finely grated

1 egg, lightly beaten

1 bag of mixed salad leaves, about 115g

10 cherry tomatoes, halved

1 lemon

1 tbsp olive oil

fine sea salt and freshly ground black pepper

FOR THE SAUCE

2 tbsp low-fat mayonnaise

1 tbsp Dijon mustard

½ tsp honey

In a medium bowl, mix together the pork, breadcrumbs, garlic, oregano, apple, egg, 1 tsp salt and ½ tsp pepper. Using your hand, bind the mixture together, ensuring all the flavours are combined.

Divide the meat mixture into 4 balls, then gently press each between the palms of your hands, creating a burger shape about 10cm in diameter. Place on a plate and chill in the fridge for at least 15 minutes, allowing the meat to become compact and making the burgers easier to cook.

Meanwhile, for the sauce, pour the mayonnaise, Dijon mustard and honey into a small bowl and mix together.

Place the salad leaves and tomatoes in a medium bowl, then season with salt and pepper and the juice of the lemon. Mix well and divide it between 4 plates.

Pour the oil into a large frying pan, and, using your fingertips, spread it over the entire base of the pan. Set it over a medium heat for 1 minute. Add the burgers and cook for 4 minutes on each side. Once cooked, place each burger on its bed of salad and top with the prepared sauce, or you can choose to top them with my amazing Apple Sauce (see page 91). So tasty!

MARINATED LAMB SKEWERS WITH PEPPERS AND RED ONIONS

SPIEDINI DI AGNELLO CON PEPERONI E CIPOLLE ROSSE

This recipe screams summer barbecues, but we make it all year round. We love lamb, and, simply cooked this way, it's so quick and tasty. You can add any vegetable of your choice, such as courgettes or mushrooms, and of course you can substitute lamb with chicken if you prefer. If you are not calorie-counting, a cheeky slice of halloumi cheese makes a nice addition, too.

SERVES 4

150g natural yogurt

2 tbsp good-quality mint sauce

2 tbsp finely chopped
    rosemary leaves

350g lean lamb, cut into 3cm cubes

1 red or orange pepper, deseeded
    and cut into 2cm pieces

1 red onion, cut into 8

fine sea salt and freshly ground
    black pepper

Pour the yogurt into a medium bowl and add the mint sauce and rosemary. Season with a large pinch each of salt and pepper. Add the lamb and mix well, ensuring that each piece is coated with the marinade. Leave to rest at room temperature for 10 minutes.

Thread the lamb on to 4 large metal skewers, alternating each piece with slices of the pepper and onion. (If you use smaller wooden skewers, please make sure that they have been soaked in water beforehand; they are also smaller, so you might find that you need to make 8 skewers.)

Preheat a griddle pan over a high heat, or a barbecue to its hottest setting.

Cook the lamb on the hot griddle pan for 8 minutes, turning the meat over every 2 minutes to ensure that every side is coloured. (If you're cooking the skewers on a barbecue, you may need slightly less cooking time.) If your griddle pan has a tall side rim, place a flat tray on top of the skewers to make sure all of the elements are touching the griddle pan and being cooked.

Serve hot, accompanied with a green salad of your choice.

SUNDAY SPECIALS

◆◆◆◆◆◆◆◆◆◆◆◆◆◆◆◆◆◆◆◆◆◆◆◆◆◆◆◆◆

I travel a lot for work, which means I can sometimes be away from my family for weeks at a time when I'm filming. It's not easy on any of us, but at the same time I know I am extremely lucky. Not only because I get to see so many amazing places, meet interesting people and learn new cooking techniques and recipes, but also because it actually means that I truly appreciate real quality time with my family when I come home.

When I'm home, we sit down as a family most evenings for dinner. I think it's so important to eat together as often as you can, I don't believe in eating in different rooms or at different times. With the boys growing up and their social lives becoming nearly as busy as my diary, it has become harder to do it as regularly as we would like, so we created the Sunday Special! As a family, we have all made a pact that we will eat at least two dinners together during the week, as well as a Sunday brunch, lunch or dinner. We make more of an effort cooking for these 'special' meals, using the recipes you will find in this chapter. These dishes are also fantastic for when you have friends over. They are not necessarily more expensive or time-consuming to make, but they are the kind of recipes that make you feel as though a little extra thought has been given for your sake, with huge amounts of love. Who doesn't want a bit of that a couple of times a week?

Family time is so important, and, for me, eating and drinking with family and friends is like a secret medicine that makes me happy. I hope so much that you enjoy some of our favourite meals with your own loved ones. Even if you are really busy and working odd hours and can only manage a Sunday Special once a month, it will be so worth it.

May the Sunday Special pact between my family – and now yours, as well – continue forever!

◆◆◆◆◆◆◆◆◆◆◆◆◆◆◆◆◆◆◆◆◆◆◆◆◆◆◆

NEAPOLITAN PIZZA

PIZZA NAPOLETANA

◆◆◆◆◆◆◆◆◆◆◆◆◆◆◆◆◆◆◆◆◆◆◆◆◆◆

I know a lot of you will look at this recipe, think it's too much hassle and just want to go and buy some pizzas instead, but it is so much fun to make them from scratch and they taste so much better too. I often make pizzas when we have another family coming over, as, once the dough is ready, they take just minutes to prepare and everyone can add their own toppings. Traditionally, Neapolitan pizza is cooked in a wood-fired pizza oven, but of course the recipe will also work in a regular oven, and I've given both methods here. I have used much less fresh yeast than you might find in other recipes, but this is not a typo! In Naples, we give the dough longer to rise, so it doesn't need as much yeast. Also, using less yeast gives a far lighter and easier-to-digest pizza base.

MAKES 10

FOR THE DOUGH
1.5kg '00' flour, plus more to dust
1.5g fresh yeast (about ½ tsp)
fine sea salt

FOR THE TOMATO SAUCE
6 x 400g cans of chopped tomatoes
30 basil leaves
10 tbsp extra virgin olive oil, plus
    more to drizzle on top

TO SERVE
10 buffalo mozzarella balls (about
    125g each), drained and cut into
    1cm cubes

First make the dough. Place the flour and 45g salt into a large bowl and mix to distribute the salt evenly. Pour 1 litre water, at room temperature, into a jug, add the yeast and stir to combine. Pour the water and yeast into the bowl of flour a little at a time, mixing everything together with the handle of a wooden spoon to create a wet dough.

Turn out the dough on to a well-floured surface and knead it with your hands for 10 minutes until smooth and elastic. Shape into a ball and return it to the large bowl. Cover with a tea towel and rest it at room temperature for 1 hour.

Lightly dust a work surface with flour and place the dough on top. Divide equally into 10 pieces and roll each piece into tight balls, making sure there are no air bubbles in the middle.

Dust 2 large trays with flour and place the balls inside, about 10cm apart from each other. Cover with a tea towel and let rest at room temperature for 5 hours.

Meanwhile, to prepare the sauce, place the tomatoes, basil, extra virgin olive oil and 4 tsp salt into a large bowl, mix all together and set aside.

continued overleaf

NEAPOLITAN PIZZA ~ CONTINUED

Fire up your pizza oven, if you have one, and make sure it reaches about 450°C. Alternatively, preheat a regular oven to its maximum setting for at least 30 minutes, placing a pizza stone inside on a middle shelf.

Gently pick up a dough ball and place on a lightly floured surface. Use your hands to push the dough ball out from the centre, creating a disc about 30cm in diameter.

Use a large kitchen spoon to spread 1½ tbsp of the tomato mixture on top of the pizza base. The best way to do this is by pouring the tomato mixture into the middle of the pizza base and spreading it from the centre going outwards, using the back of a large spoon. Leave a 1cm border clean.

Scatter a chopped mozzarella ball over the tomato mixture and evenly drizzle over 2 tbsp extra virgin olive oil. If using a pizza oven, gently pick up the pizza with a pizza shovel and cook in the middle of the oven for 30 seconds. Turn the pizza and cook for a further 30 seconds. A traditional Neapolitan pizza should cook in less than 1 minute in a wood-fired pizza oven. If using a regular oven, transfer the pizza to the hot pizza stone; it should be cooked in 4 minutes.

Continue to shape, top and cook your remaining pizzas and enjoy the Neapolitan experience.

SUPER-SPICY PIZZA

PIZZA SUPER PICCANTE CON 'NDUJA CALABRESE

◆◆◆◆◆◆◆◆◆◆◆◆◆◆◆◆◆◆◆◆◆◆◆◆◆◆◆◆

There is nothing quite like making your own pizzas and your kids getting involved, and this recipe is a tribute to all the toppings my nineteen-year-old son Luciano loves. We were filming near Tropea in Capo Vaticano at Mr Agostino Pontorieno's farm when we put this amazing pizza together. 'Nduja is a spreadable *salumi* which is made from pork fat, Calabrian peppers and herbs and spices. The peppers give 'nduja its powerful spice kick and its iconic red colour. It has a fantastic unique flavour that all of us love and I'm sure you will too. You can use 2 tbsp caramelised onions from a jar to make this simpler and quicker if you don't want to caramelise your own onions. It's a great recipe for using up the last of any dough and sauce from a big pizza-making session!

MAKES 1

2 tbsp extra virgin olive oil

1 large tropea or red onion, finely sliced

1 tsp caster sugar

1 ball Neapolitan Pizza Dough (see page 128)

2–3 tbsp Tomato Sauce (see page 128)

½ tsp chilli flakes

8 slices of spicy salami

125g buffalo mozzarella ball, torn

5 tsp 'nduja

fine sea salt

To caramelise the onions, take 1 tbsp of the olive oil and put it into a small frying pan over a medium-low heat. Fry the onion for about 8 minutes until translucent, then add the sugar and a pinch of salt and continue to cook over a low heat for 15–20 minutes until caramelised and sweet.

Prepare the pizza base (see pages 128 and 131). Smear on the tomato sauce, then add the chilli flakes. Top with the slices of spicy salami, then the torn mozzarella, being sure to place some on top of the salami slices so it melts into it.

Top with the caramelised onions and 'nduja and drizzle over the remaining 1 tbsp oil. Place into a wood-fired pizza oven, or a preheated conventional oven, and cook as on page 131; in a wood-fired oven it will only take 1 minute, or about 4 minutes in a regular oven.

ITALIAN BUCK'S FIZZ

COCKTAIL FRIZZANTINO

On Christmas morning, and birthdays, I wake up my wife with this, my version of a buck's fizz, and we continue to drink it throughout the day. The colour is amazing and so festive and the combination of the spirits with the prosecco are a match made in heaven. A drink to mark any occasion, or even just because – please try it, you won't be disappointed!

SERVES 6–8

plenty of ice cubes

100ml Campari

100ml Cointreau

100ml fresh orange juice

750ml prosecco

orange slices and redcurrants,
   to serve

Put plenty of ice into a large jug, then add the Campari, Cointreau and orange juice and mix well.

Top with the prosecco and serve immediately in glasses garnished with orange slices and redcurrants.

SPICY AUBERGINE BAKE WITH MOZZARELLA AND PECORINO CHEESE

MELANZANE PICCANTI AL FORNO CON MOZZARELLA E PECORINO

◆◆◆◆◆◆◆◆◆◆◆◆◆◆◆◆◆◆◆◆◆◆◆◆◆

It's true that everyone loves the dishes their mothers made for them when they were growing up, but I can honestly say that my mother's *melanzane alla Parmigiana* was the best ever. Even though I make it exactly like she showed me, it's still not the same… or maybe it is and it's just the memories I have that made hers so special. Normally, I make this with canned chopped tomatoes, fresh mozzarella and Parmesan, but I wanted to give this version a little kick with pecorino cheese and chilli. Feel free to add a bit more chilli oil if you like the heat, or you can substitute the pecorino with Grana Padano.

SERVES 6–8

6 large aubergines (about 2kg in total)
5 eggs
150g plain flour
300ml olive oil
350g grated mozzarella cheese
150g finely grated pecorino cheese
sea salt flakes

FOR THE SAUCE
4 tbsp olive oil
1 large onion, finely chopped
1.4 litres tomato passata
4 tbsp chilli oil, or to taste
20 basil leaves
250g mascarpone cheese
fine sea salt and freshly ground
   black pepper

Slice the aubergines lengthways into slices about 2.5mm thick. Place in a sieve, sprinkle over some sea salt flakes and leave over the sink for 1 hour to allow any excess liquid to drain from the aubergines. We use salt flakes here to draw out the moisture, as fine salt would be absorbed into the aubergines.

In the meantime, to prepare the sauce, place the 4 tbsp of olive oil and the onion in a large shallow saucepan and fry over a medium heat for 8 minutes, occasionally stirring with a wooden spoon. Pour in the passata and chilli oil, then add the basil, 1½ tsp fine salt and 1 tsp pepper and stir for 2 minutes. Add the mascarpone, stir to combine all the ingredients, then reduce the heat slightly and leave to simmer for 10 minutes. Taste: this is the time to add in a bit more chilli oil if you want a stronger kick. Set aside.

Preheat the oven to 180°C/fan 160°C/Gas 4.

Put the aubergine slices on to some kitchen paper and pat dry. Place the eggs, 1 tsp fine salt and ½ tsp pepper into a medium bowl and beat well. Pour the flour on to a medium flat tray. Dip each aubergine slice into the flour and then into the egg to coat all over.

Heat 10 tbsp of the olive oil into a large frying pan and fry the aubergine slices until golden on both sides, about 2 minutes each side. You will need to work in batches. (Depending on the size of your frying pan, it should take about 6 batches.)

Transfer the slices on to kitchen paper to drain off any excess oil. After 3 batches have been browned, add the remaining olive oil to your frying pan and heat until very hot. Continue to fry the remaining aubergine slices, again transferring them on to kitchen paper to drain the excess oil.

Layer one-third of the aubergine in a rectangular oven dish, measuring about 30 x 25cm. Spoon 3 ladles of the tomato sauce on top. Sprinkle over 100g mozzarella and 50g pecorino. Repeat the process twice more. You'll have a little more than 3 ladles left of the tomato sauce and 50g mozzarella to make a last layer; this extra sauce on top is absorbed through the dish while it cooks and keeps it extra-moist. Sprinkle over a pinch of pepper and cover with foil.

Bake in the oven for 20 minutes. Remove the foil from the oven dish and continue to bake for a further 30 minutes. Remove from the oven and allow to rest for about 5 minutes before portioning. Serve with some crusty ciabatta bread and salad. Just like mamma used to make.

pictured overleaf

THREE-BEAN CHILLI SHEPHERD'S PIE

PASTICCIO SALATO CON FAGIOLI E PUREA DI PATATE

◆◆◆◆◆◆◆◆◆◆◆◆◆◆◆◆◆◆◆◆◆◆◆◆◆

I came up with this recipe during the horrible Coronavirus isolation days, at a time when I was in Italy and away from my family for over a month, not able to get a flight home. For a couple of days, I only had storecupboard supplies and vegetables from my garden, but I knew, with those, that I was one of the lucky ones. I really fancied a meal with strong flavours, with the comfort food feel of my home in the UK, and this recipe didn't disappoint. As soon as I came home, I made it for everyone. I feel very lucky to have finally been able to share it with my family and I hope you enjoy it as much as we did.

SERVES 4–6

FOR THE TOPPING

1.2kg potatoes, roughly chopped

50ml whole milk

100g salted butter, cut into roughly 4cm cubes

70g grated mozzarella

fine sea salt and freshly ground black pepper

FOR THE FILLING

4 tbsp olive oil

1 large onion, finely chopped

200g baby aubergines, sliced into 1cm circles, then circles cut into quarters

1 large courgette, finely chopped

1 tbsp tomato purée

1 tsp ground cumin

1 tsp ground coriander

1 tsp cayenne pepper

1 tsp paprika

400g can of black beans, drained

400g can of borlotti beans, drained

400g can of red kidney beans in chilli, DO NOT drain!

For the topping, fill a large saucepan with 3 litres of water, add 1 tbsp salt and the potatoes and boil over a high heat for 30 minutes. Drain, and, using a potato ricer, mash them. Add 1 tsp salt, ½ tsp pepper, the milk and butter and stir with a wooden spoon to create a creamy mash. Set aside.

Preheat the oven to 200°C/fan 180°C/Gas 6.

Pour the oil into a large shallow saucepan and place over a medium heat. Place in the onion and fry for 3 minutes. Add the aubergines, courgette, 1 tsp salt and ½ tsp pepper and fry for 10 minutes, stirring occasionally with a wooden spoon. Spoon in the tomato purée, cumin, coriander, cayenne and paprika and stir to combine. Fry for a further 8 minutes, stirring occasionally. Pour in the beans along with the chilli-flavoured juice of the red kidney beans and stir. Cook for a further 2 minutes, then remove from the heat and pour into a large oven dish (mine was about 27 x 20 x 6cm).

Spoon over the creamy mash and sprinkle the top with the grated mozzarella cheese. Place in the middle of the oven for 15 minutes. Finally, put your pie under a preheated grill for 2 minutes, allowing the cheese to slightly brown. Serve up immediately. Honestly, this dish is delicious and is a must-try.

VEGETABLE AND ROSEMARY STACK

TORRETTA DI VERDURE CON MOZZARELLA DI BUFALA E OLIO AL ROSMARINO

◆◆◆◆◆◆◆◆◆◆◆◆◆◆◆◆◆◆◆◆◆◆◆◆◆◆◆◆

There are many 'blue zones' in Italy where the population's average age is well into the 90s, with many people living to over 100. I took my in-laws Elizabeth and Malcolm (who are a very young 75 years of age) to Acciaroli to find out the secrets of a long life. We were met by Annamaria, a 78-year-old 'tour guide', who explained that a little walk every day, good-quality fresh ingredients and a little glass of wine every now and then was the secret to a healthy long life. This vegetable stack is the perfect way to start that life and why not accompany it with a cheeky glass of white or rosé wine? If it works for Annamaria...

SERVES 4

100ml olive oil, plus 30ml more
  for frying

4 rosemary sprigs

3 garlic cloves, crushed and peeled
  but left whole

100g cherry tomatoes, halved

1 large red pepper

1 courgette

1 aubergine

250g buffalo mozzarella balls

50g Parmesan cheese, shaved

8 basil leaves

100g sliced marinated aubergines

fine sea salt and freshly ground
  black pepper

Put the 100ml of olive oil in a small saucepan with the rosemary and garlic. Turn the heat to medium and allow the oil, rosemary and garlic to warm up together and infuse until just starting to sizzle. Remove from the heat, add the tomatoes and set aside.

Heat a griddle pan over a high heat.

Cut the pepper into 3–4 large pieces, removing and discarding the ribs and seeds. Season the inside part of each piece with salt and then place on the hot griddle to cook. Slice the courgette into pieces about half the width of your finger, on a diagonal. Season with salt on both sides and then lay the slices on the griddle along with the pepper to grill. Every so often, brush the vegetables with the infused oil from the tomatoes so they take on that incredible flavour. Turn the pepper and courgettes after a couple of minutes, when they have got nicely charred, but before they burn.

Slice the aubergine widthways into even slices about as thick as your finger – you should get 4–5 pieces.

Place a large frying pan over a medium-high heat and add the remaining 30ml of olive oil. Season with salt and lay the aubergine slices gently into the hot oil to fry. When golden on one side, turn and fry on the other. When the slices are cooked, remove from the heat.

Slice the mozzarella into 4 slices and drain it well on a couple of sheets of kitchen paper.

Build your stacks: place a fried aubergine slice on each of 4 large plates. Top with a couple of Parmesan shavings and 2 basil leaves. Add a slice of mozzarella, some more Parmesan and a grinding of black pepper. Top with 2–3 slices of courgette, followed by a little bit more Parmesan. Cut the pepper pieces in half to a similar size as the stack and then place one on top, followed by a generous spoonful of the marinated aubergines.

Finish the plate by placing a few of the marinated tomatoes around the stack, dressing with their delicious oil. Add the rosemary sprigs and serve.

pictured overleaf

LOBSTER CATALAN-STYLE WITH CHERRY TOMATOES AND RED ONIONS

ARAGOSTA ALLA CATALANA

◆◆◆◆◆◆◆◆◆◆◆◆◆◆◆◆◆◆◆◆◆◆◆◆◆

I am very lucky to be able to come away with my family to Sardinia for most Christmases. To be honest, roast pork is my go-to for Christmas Day, but it has now become a bit of a tradition to go to the beach either on Christmas Eve or Boxing Day and cook this lobster recipe. Being by the sea, the fish is so fresh – we went to the beach and cooked lobster one year just for fun and it has now become a D'Acampo custom. This dish is perfect after a heavy Christmas meal from the day before, but I'll make up any excuse I can to eat it any month of the year!

SERVES 6–8

4 live lobsters (about 800g each)

700g new potatoes

300g green beans

150g cherry tomatoes, quartered

1 red onion, finely sliced

2 tbsp finely chopped flat leaf parsley leaves

4 tbsp capers in brine, drained

100g Taggiasche olives, pitted

juice of 2 lemons

140ml olive oil

fine sea salt

Bring a very large pan of salted water to the boil – there needs to be enough water for the lobsters to be completely submerged. Humanely kill the lobsters by inserting a knife between the shell of the head and the body. Submerge in the water and par-boil for 7–8 minutes. Remove and chill immediately with some ice before removing the heads and splitting the tails in half lengthways.

For the salad, boil the new potatoes until tender, then quarter them. Blanch the green beans in boiling water for 2 minutes, then drain and immediately plunge into iced water, to halt the cooking and keep them bright green. Gently mix the potatoes and green beans together in a bowl with the tomatoes, onion, parsley, capers and olives. In a small bowl or cup, mix the juice of 1 lemon with 60ml of the olive oil and set aside.

Heat a griddle pan over a high heat. Mix the remaining 80ml of olive oil and the juice of the remaining lemon with ½ tsp salt, then brush over the flesh of the lobsters. Put the lobsters meat-side down on the griddle and cook for 4–5 minutes until caramelised and cooked.

Take the lobster meat from the shells, along with any claw meat, roughly chop it and then add to the salad, but don't discard the shells. Dress the salad with the lemon dressing, tossing gently. Lay the lobster shells on a plate, then refill them with your delicious salad. Serve immediately.

BAKED SEA BASS IN THYME-FLAVOURED SALT CRUST

SPIGOLA AL FORNO IN CROSTA DI SALE E TIMO

◆◆◆◆◆◆◆◆◆◆◆◆◆◆◆◆◆◆◆◆◆◆◆◆◆◆

This is such a wonderful recipe that looks so impressive when serving to guests, but I must admit, when I'm making this for my family, I do use a larger fish than I suggest here, about 1.4kg. We just love it so much! I've suggested a 1kg fish as it's less costly, but you will probably need to serve it with potatoes or roasted veg as well. Whatever size of fish you choose, I recommend you make my Brussels Sprouts and Chorizo or Simple Spicy Spinach with Garlic and Olive Oil (see pages 88 and 89) to go with it.

SERVES 4

1kg whole sea bass, gutted and cleaned (but not scaled), with head, tail and skin on

1.5kg rock salt

4 tbsp thyme leaves

100g bag of crispy mixed salad leaves

FOR THE DRESSING

100ml extra virgin olive oil

juice of 1 large lemon

2 tbsp chopped flat leaf parsley leaves

fine sea salt and freshly ground black pepper

Preheat the oven to 200°C/fan 180°C/Gas 6.

Wash and clean the fish under cold tap water. Please do not remove the scales, as they will protect the fish while it is baking in the salt crust.

Arrange a 5mm-thick layer of rock salt on a baking tray roughly the same size as the fish. I tend to lay the fish in the tray diagonally, ensuring it fits well. (You can trim the tail a bit if it doesn't quite fit.)

Pour the rest of the salt into a large bowl with the thyme. Mix in 10 tbsp cold water to moisten but not over-wet the salt, and stir. You need to create a stiff slush that can be patted into shape.

Cover the fish with the flavoured salt; it should be completely encased in the salt crust.

Bake in the middle of the oven for 30 minutes.

Meanwhile, pour the olive oil and lemon juice into a small bowl and sprinkle on the parsley. Season with salt and pepper and whisk all together to create a dressing. Set aside.

To serve the fish, crack open the salt crust with a spoon and lift away any large pieces. Use a pastry brush to sweep away any remaining salt.

Peel the skin off the sea bass, pulling it away with a fork. Lift the skin up, remove and discard.

Run the tip of the fork down the centre of the fish, just to one side of the spine. Gently lift the first fillet on to a warmed plate. Do the same on the other side. Turn the fish over and repeat the process, or lift away the spine and take the other fillets that way, if you find it easier.

Once all the fillets are on the plates, drizzle over three-quarters of the prepared dressing. Serve immediately with the crispy mixed salad leaves tossed with the remaining lemon dressing.

pictured overleaf

ITALIAN CHICKEN CORDON BLEU WITH CHEESY MUSTARD SAUCE

POLLO RIPIENO DI PROSCIUTTO, CON SALSA DI SENAPE E FORMAGGIO

◆◆◆◆◆◆◆◆◆◆◆◆◆◆◆◆◆◆◆◆◆◆◆◆◆◆◆◆◆

My entire family love chicken, veal or pork Milanese, where the meat is coated in breadcrumbs and then fried. This recipe came about years ago, after my boys asked for that so often that I wanted to try something a bit different. Inspired by the traditional Cordon Bleu idea of meat wrapped around cheese and ham, it has a cheesy sauce, which you pour over yourself, so you can have as much or as little as you want. It was a huge success and is now a firm D'Acampo family favourite. Substitute the ham for Parma ham if you prefer, and you can go as cheesy as you like once you feel comfortable with the method.

SERVES 4

FOR THE CHICKEN

4 large skinless chicken breast fillets, about 250g each

4 slices of ham, about 35g each

250g fine dried breadcrumbs

4 eggs

fine sea salt and freshly ground black pepper

FOR THE SAUCE

30g salted butter

1 tbsp plain flour

300ml whole milk

2 tsp English mustard

60g grated Parmesan cheese

100g grated Cheddar cheese

Place a chicken breast on a chopping board and put one hand on top of it to keep it steady. Insert a sharp knife in the middle of the thickest part and make a slit about 5cm long, running the knife into the breast until it is three-quarters of the way through, creating a pocket. Open up the breast and put a sheet of cling film on top. Very gently (making sure you do not split the chicken) bash down the meat with a meat mallet or rolling pin until the breasts are about 5mm thick. Remove the cling film, season with a pinch of salt and pepper and place a slice of ham on one side of the chicken. Fold the other side over the ham and close the chicken around it.

Put a sheet of cling film, about 35 x 30cm, on a work surface. Place the chicken at one end. Grab both sides of the cling film and roll away from you 2–3 times: you want to encase the chicken tightly, but keep it flat, don't roll it into a spiral. Chill for at least 1 hour. Repeat to stuff and wrap all the chicken.

Preheat the oven to 180°C/fan 160°C/Gas 4. Place the breadcrumbs on a baking tray, season well and mix. Toast in the oven for 5 minutes. Remove and allow to cool.

Increase the oven temperature to 200°C/fan 180°C/Gas 6 and line a large flat oven tray with baking parchment.

Break the eggs into a medium bowl with 1 tsp salt and 1 tsp pepper and gently whisk all together.

continued overleaf

ITALIAN CHICKEN CORDON BLEU WITH CHEESY MUSTARD SAUCE ~ CONTINUED

Take one breast at a time. Remove the cling film and coat first in the breadcrumbs, then gently shake off any excess. Immediately immerse the breast into the eggs, making sure the meat is covered by the eggs, and again coat in the breadcrumbs. Place the chicken breast on the lined oven tray. Repeat the process with all 4 breasts. Season with a pinch of salt and pepper and cook in the oven for 40 minutes.

In the meantime, to create the cheese sauce, melt the butter in a small saucepan over a medium heat. Add the flour and mix together using a hand-held whisk for about 1 minute. Pour in the milk slowly, continuously stirring with the whisk for 2 minutes. Stir in the mustard and cook for another minute. Tip in the Parmesan and continue to stir, ensuring the cheese has melted (1–2 minutes). Add the Cheddar, again continuously stirring to make sure no lumps are formed. The sauce will start to thicken. Season with salt and pepper to taste and remove from the heat until ready. (If the sauce cools down too much before the chicken is cooked, just return it to the heat for a couple of minutes, constantly stirring, to reheat it.) Pour the sauce into a warmed jug.

Place the chicken breasts on warmed plates and drizzle over the cheesy mustard sauce, or serve it on the side for everyone to help themselves. Serve with creamy mash, and any greens of your choice.

LASAGNE WITH A SUCCULENT LAMB RAGÙ

LASAGNE CON RAGÙ DI AGNELLO

◆◆◆◆◆◆◆◆◆◆◆◆◆◆◆◆◆◆◆◆◆◆◆◆

I absolutely love a good lasagne, it offers you everything in one dish: protein, calcium, vegetables and carbs. There is nothing better after being out and about on a Sunday – especially after standing in a field watching one of your kids in a match – than coming home to a beautiful lasagne ready for you in the oven. I have used minced lamb in this recipe for a change, but of course traditional minced beef – or even a combination of beef and pork – is also lovely. If you decide to prepare the lasagne in the morning, or the day before, refrigerate it when it has cooled slightly, but return it to room temperature again before you bake it in the oven.

SERVES 4–6

FOR THE MEAT SAUCE
4 tbsp olive oil
1 courgette, finely chopped
1 large onion, finely chopped
1 carrot, finely chopped
500g minced lamb
50ml red wine
1 tbsp tomato purée
1 tbsp Worcestershire sauce
400g can of chopped tomatoes
fine sea salt and freshly ground
   black pepper

FOR THE CHEESE SAUCE
100g salted butter
100g plain flour
1 litre whole milk
1 tsp freshly grated nutmeg
100g finely grated Parmesan cheese

TO ASSEMBLE
12 dried lasagne sheets
20g finely grated Parmesan cheese

Place a large, shallow saucepan over a medium heat with the oil and vegetables and fry for 15 minutes, occasionally stirring with a wooden spoon. Add the lamb and stir, breaking up the meat with the spoon so it browns all over, cooking for about 2 minutes. Pour in the wine and stir for 2 minutes. Add the tomato purée, Worcestershire sauce, tomatoes, 2 tsp salt and ½ tsp pepper. Stir, reduce the heat slightly and simmer for 25 minutes. Preheat the oven to 200°C/fan 180°C/Gas 6.

In the meantime, melt the butter in a saucepan, slowly pour in the flour and stir vigorously with a hand-held whisk, creating a paste. Pour in half the milk, stirring until the paste combines with the milk. Pour in the rest of the milk, still stirring. Once the sauce is smooth, add the nutmeg, the 100g of Parmesan, 1 tsp salt and ½ tsp pepper. Stir with the whisk over a medium heat until the bechamel thickens, about 6 minutes.

Cover the base of an oven dish – measuring about 30 x 25cm – with 4 lasagne sheets. Spoon half the meat sauce on top. Pour one-third of the bechamel over. Place 4 more lasagne sheets on the bechamel, followed by the rest of the meat, then half the remaining bechamel. Lay the last 4 lasagne sheets on top and pour over the rest of the bechamel. Sprinkle over the 20g of Parmesan and bake for 30 minutes.

Let the lasagne rest for 5 minutes before portioning. For me, there's no need to add anything other than a nice cold beer.

BRAISED LAMB SHANKS IN HONEY AND RED WINE SAUCE

STINCO DI AGNELLO AL VINO ROSSO E MIELE

◆◆◆◆◆◆◆◆◆◆◆◆◆◆◆◆◆◆◆◆◆◆◆◆◆

Casseroles are usually made in the colder weather, but in our house we enjoy this dish all year round. It is one of those Sunday Specials which is also great for a dinner party and will always be received with great excitement. I think it's because not many people make it and yet it is really easy to do, and – as it's in the oven most of the time – it leaves you time to spend with your guests. The taste is amazing and the meat becomes so soft it just melts in the mouth. As with my roast chicken recipe, you will see I have added strawberry jam; it's not a typo, I promise! The sweetness works perfectly, trust me.

SERVES 4

4 large lamb shanks, about 600g each

2 celery sticks, each cut into 3

1 onion, cut into chunks

4 rosemary sprigs

10 whole peppercorns

1 bottle of good-quality red wine

3 red onions, quartered

2 tbsp balsamic glaze

2 tbsp honey

2 tbsp strawberry jam

1 tbsp good-quality mint sauce

Place the lamb in a large casserole dish with the celery, onion, rosemary and peppercorns. Pour over the wine, cover and marinate in the fridge for 5 hours, basting after 2½ hours. Take the shanks out of the fridge 20 minutes before you are ready to cook them.

Preheat the oven to 190°C/fan 170°C/Gas 5.

Place the casserole dish over a medium heat and bring to the boil, cover with the lid, then put into the preheated oven for 1 hour. Remove the casserole dish, baste the meat with the juices and return to the oven with the lid on at a slight angle, allowing the sauce to thicken. Continue to cook for 1 hour.

Remove the casserole dish from the oven, take the lamb shanks out of the cooking liquid and place in a roasting tray. Spoon over 4 ladles of the cooking liquid to keep the meat moist and add the red onions around the shanks. Drizzle over the balsamic glaze and honey.

Return the lamb to the oven and roast for 25–30 minutes or until the meat starts to fall off the bone, basting occasionally.

Meanwhile, strain the remaining cooking liquid from the casserole dish into a small saucepan, add the jam and mint sauce, and place over a low heat, cooking until its volume has reduced by half.

Serve the amazing lamb shanks with vegetables and creamy mash. Don't forget to smother it all with the delicious gravy.

CRISPY BREADED PORK CHOPS WITH ROSEMARY

COTOLETTA DI MAIALE ALLA MILANESE

◆◆◆◆◆◆◆◆◆◆◆◆◆◆◆◆◆◆◆◆◆◆◆◆◆◆◆◆◆

Nothing can beat a Milanese-style hunk of meat, fish, or even vegetable – we all love that crispy breadcrumb coating. Pork is probably my favourite meat to cook Milanese-style; its sweetness works really well with the rosemary here, and I heartily recommend serving it with a cold Italian beer. If you prefer, you can try the same recipe with chicken or veal instead. *Buon Appetito!*

SERVES 4

4 bone-in pork chops,
   250–300g each

3 eggs

150g fine dried breadcrumbs

3 tbsp finely chopped
   rosemary leaves

250ml olive oil

fine sea salt and freshly ground
   black pepper

Place the pork chops on a chopping board, and, with a sharp knife, cut 2 slits into the fat; this will ensure the chops don't curl up during cooking. Place the chops in between 2 sheets of cling film, and, using a meat mallet or a rolling pin, bash down the meat until each chop is about 1cm thick. Set aside.

Break the eggs into a large bowl with 1 tsp salt and ½ tsp pepper and gently whisk with a fork. Place the breadcrumbs on a medium flat tray and mix in the chopped rosemary.

Take one chop at a time and first coat in the breadcrumbs on both sides. Gently shake off any excess. Immediately immerse the chop into the eggs, making sure both meat and bone are covered, then again coat in the breadcrumbs. Place the pork chop on a chopping board, and, with the palm of your hand, slightly press down the meat part to get the meat in shape. Coat all the pork chops in the same way.

Pour the olive oil into a large frying pan and place over a medium heat. Take a pinch of breadcrumbs and sprinkle them into the oil: if they start to sizzle, the oil is hot enough.

Cook the pork chops, 2 at a time, for 4 minutes on each side to have medium-cooked meat, if you prefer your meat medium-well done, fry for 1 minute longer on each side. You are looking for a golden/light brown colour all over.

Drain the crispy chops on kitchen paper and sprinkle over a little salt. I love this meal with a crisp salad, simply dressed with extra virgin olive oil, salt and lemon juice, or some seasonal vegetables, but the kids always insist they are served with mustard mash, which is also *fantastico*.

CANNELLONI STUFFED WITH COURGETTES, PEPPERS AND MASCARPONE

CANNELLONI RIPIENI DI ZUCCHINE, PEPERONI E MASCARPONE

◆◆◆◆◆◆◆◆◆◆◆◆◆◆◆◆◆◆◆◆◆◆◆◆◆◆◆

Ricotta and spinach cannelloni is such a lovely classic Italian dish, but sometimes it's nice to have a change. This recipe came about when I was hosting a working lunch at home; two of my guests were vegetarians and I wanted to offer them something they may not have had before. They absolutely loved it, so I decided to try it on the kids later that week, and, to my delight, they loved it too. Win-win for everyone, work or play!

SERVES 4

2 large courgettes, very finely chopped into tiny cubes

1 large onion, finely chopped

1 red or orange pepper, very finely chopped into tiny cubes

4 tbsp olive oil

2 x 400g cans of chopped tomatoes

6 tbsp extra virgin olive oil

100ml double cream

10 basil leaves

250g mascarpone cheese

100g finely grated Parmesan cheese

16 fresh egg lasagne sheets

fine sea salt and freshly ground black pepper

In a large shallow saucepan or frying pan, fry the courgettes, onion and pepper in the regular olive oil over a high heat for 15 minutes, until soft. Season with 1 tsp salt, or to taste, and ½ tsp pepper, place in a large bowl and set aside.

Preheat the oven to 200°C/fan 180°C/Gas 6.

Pour the canned tomatoes into a medium jug with the extra virgin olive oil, cream, basil leaves and 1 tsp salt, or to taste, and gently stir to combine. Pour a large ladle of this sauce into a baking dish measuring about 30 x 25cm, spread it out to cover the base and set aside.

Take the bowl of fried vegetables and stir in the mascarpone and 70g of the Parmesan cheese. Lay the lasagne sheets on a work surface and divide the mascarpone mixture between them. Roll up the sheets to secure the filling.

Place the cannelloni seam-sides down in a single layer on top of the sauce in the baking dish. Pour over the remaining tomato sauce and sprinkle over the remaining Parmesan.

Bake in the preheated oven for 30 minutes. Once ready, allow to rest out of the oven for 5 minutes, then portion and serve with your favourite salad.

TRADITIONAL NEAPOLITAN PASTA WITH SLOW-COOKED ONION AND MEAT SAUCE

PASTA ALLA GENOVESE

◆◆◆◆◆◆◆◆◆◆◆◆◆◆◆◆◆◆◆◆◆◆◆◆◆◆◆

This recipe is dedicated to my brother-in-law Orlando di Franco who always requests it when he comes to visit. Now I know you might scan this recipe and think you can't be bothered to make something that is going to take hours… but please trust me, it is worth your time and only needs you to give it a quick stir every so often. I promise you won't regret it. When cooking the onions, remember to stir every ten minutes so they don't burn. You want a sweet, creamy texture, so slowly but surely is the only way for this dish. You can cook the sauce the day before if you prefer, which makes the flavours even better!

SERVES 6

15 large onions, halved and finely sliced

2 vegetable stock cubes

10 tbsp olive oil

500g pork fillet, cut into 4cm cubes

400g beef fillet, cut into 4cm cubes

750g dried paccheri (large tubes) or rigatoni pasta

6 tbsp finely grated pecorino cheese

fine sea salt and freshly ground black pepper

Place the onions, crumbled stock cubes, oil, 2 tbsp salt and 1 tsp pepper into an extra-large saucepan. Cook over a medium-low heat for 20 minutes, stirring occasionally.

Reduce the heat to a minimum and cook for 40 minutes. Stir every 10 minutes, ensuring the onions don't burn. Boil the kettle, pour in 500ml just-boiled water, stir and cook for 1 hour, stirring every 10–15 minutes. Pour over a further 500ml just-boiled water, stir and cook for 1 hour more, stirring every 10–15 minutes. Turn off the heat, cover and set aside to rest for 1 hour. Bring the meat to room temperature.

Take off the lid of the onion pan and pour in another 500ml just-boiled water. Mix in the meat and cook over a very low heat for 2 hours, stirring occasionally. Stir in a final 500ml just-boiled water and cook for a final hour.

Meanwhile, pour 5 litres of water with 1½ tbsp salt into a large saucepan and bring to the boil. Place in the paccheri and cook for 1 minute less than instructed on the packet for that perfect al dente bite. Drain and place the pasta into the incredible Genovese sauce. Mix well, ensuring you coat the pasta completely in the sauce.

Equally portion out the pasta for your guests on warmed plates and sprinkle 1 tbsp of pecorino cheese over each. So worth the trouble, I promise!

CRUSHED POTATO PIE WITH BEEF, GARLIC AND BASIL

SFORMATO DI PATATE CON CARNE, AGLIO E BASILICO

◆◆◆◆◆◆◆◆◆◆◆◆◆◆◆◆◆◆◆◆◆◆◆◆◆

For me, this is a perfect Sunday lunch, especially if you have been out the night before. It's tasty, filling and especially perfect on those rainy days (let's be honest, we have a lot of those here in the UK). What I really love about this recipe – other than the fantastic different textures – is that you can prepare it the day before. If you do choose to do this, take it out of the fridge and bring it to room temperature before you bake it. Also, don't panic if some of your potatoes have become softer than al dente after boiling: you are trying to create a textured mash, so it really doesn't matter.

SERVES 4–6

FOR THE TOPPING

2kg potatoes, cut into roughly 2cm cubes

150g slightly salted butter, cut into roughly 4cm cubes

100g finely grated Parmesan cheese

fine sea salt and freshly ground black pepper

FOR THE FILLING

6 tbsp olive oil

4 garlic cloves, crushed

1kg minced beef

100ml red wine

2 x 400g cans of chopped tomatoes

10 basil leaves

For the topping, fill a large saucepan with 3 litres of water, add 1 tbsp salt and the cubed potatoes, switch on the heat to medium and set a timer for 25 minutes, or until the potatoes have softened to a nearly al dente bite. Drain the potatoes.

Put the butter cubes into the hot saucepan. Pour in the potatoes, and, using a wooden spoon, gently stir, coating them in the butter. Pour in half the Parmesan and again stir gently to create a crushed, textured mashed potato effect. Set aside.

In the meantime, pour the oil and garlic for the filling into a shallow saucepan and place over a medium heat. As soon as the garlic starts to sizzle, add the beef and fry for 8 minutes, breaking the meat up with a wooden spoon to allow it to brown all over. Increase the heat, pour over the wine and cook for a further 2 minutes. Pour in the tomatoes, then add the basil, 2 tsp salt and 1 tsp pepper. Stir, then reduce the heat and simmer for 35 minutes, stirring occasionally.

Preheat the oven to 200°C/fan 180°C/Gas 6.

Pour the meat sauce into a rectangular ovenproof dish (mine was 30 x 20 x 6cm). Gently spread the crushed potatoes on top. Sprinkle over the remaining Parmesan and 1 tsp pepper.

Bake in the preheated oven for 20 minutes, then let rest for 5 minutes. Serve with my amazing Simple Spicy Spinach with Garlic and Olive Oil (see page 89).

MIA'S MEATBALLS (AND MEATBALL PANINIS)

LE POLPETTE DI MIA (E PANINO CON POLPETTE)

◆◆◆◆◆◆◆◆◆◆◆◆◆◆◆◆◆◆◆◆◆◆◆◆◆

This is one of my daughter Mia's favourite recipes, not only to eat but to make. Often you will find us on a Sunday morning preparing this dish together; I have to say it is my favourite time of the week when that happens. The meatballs will be the best you have ever tasted and the secret is definitely the bread soaked in milk, it makes them so tender. I have suggested serving these with pasta, but it also works well with rice, or any leftovers are amazing in a panini.

SERVES 4

FOR THE MEATBALLS

2 tbsp olive oil

5 slices of white or brown bread, crusts discarded

200ml milk (whatever you have in the fridge is fine)

500g minced pork

250g minced beef

2 tbsp finely chopped flat leaf parsley leaves

1 large garlic clove, crushed

70g finely grated pecorino cheese

1 egg

500g fresh egg tagliatelle or fettuccine pasta

fine sea salt and freshly ground black pepper

FOR THE SAUCE

6 tbsp olive oil

1 large garlic clove, crushed

3 x 400g cans of chopped tomatoes

8 large basil leaves, torn in half

2 mozzarella balls (125g each), drained, cut into small cubes and refrigerated

Take a medium flat tray and pour in the olive oil. Using your fingertips, spread the oil all over the tray and set aside.

Break the bread into a large bowl and pour over the milk. Using your fingertips, mix the bread and milk together, to make a wet paste. Add the minced meats and combine. Now add the parsley, garlic, pecorino, 2 tsp salt and ½ tsp pepper, crack in the egg and use your hand to mix it all together.

Divide into 10 large meatballs, rolling between your palms for 30–40 seconds to become compact. Gently place on the prepared tray. Cover with cling film and rest in the fridge for 30 minutes. (You can leave them overnight if you wish.)

Now for the sauce. Place a large saucepan over a medium heat and pour in the olive oil. Place in 8 meatballs and fry for 15 minutes, gently turning regularly using 2 tablespoons, ensuring they are browned all over. (Set aside the remaining 2 meatballs for the sauce.) Switch off the heat and gently transfer the cooked meatballs one by one to a large plate, leaving the oil and juices in the saucepan.

Place the same saucepan back over a medium heat and add the remaining 2 raw meatballs. Add the crushed garlic, and, using a wooden spoon, break the meatballs into small pieces and fry in the sizzling oil for 4 minutes. Pour in the chopped tomatoes, torn basil leaves, 2 tsp salt and ½ tsp pepper. Fill one can with hot water and pour it into the saucepan. Stir, then simmer for 10 minutes, stirring occasionally and making sure you scrape the base of the pan for any caramelised bits.

Reduce the heat to a minimum and carefully place the whole meatballs in the sauce, pouring in any juices left on the plate. Gently stir, making sure the meatballs are completely covered in sauce. Cook for 2 hours, stirring occasionally, always gently, so you don't break the meatballs. Switch off the heat.

Fill a large saucepan with 4 litres of water and 1 tbsp salt and bring to the boil. Add the pasta and cook until al dente, normally 1 minute less than instructed on the packet. Meanwhile, carefully remove the meatballs from the sauce and keep warm. (If serving with rice, you don't need to remove the meatballs, you can just spoon them on the rice.)

Drain the pasta and tip into the sauce. Stir for about 20 seconds, ensuring the pasta is well coated. Divide the pasta and meatballs between 4 warmed plates, with the sauce, and sprinkle over the mozzarella. Enjoy – yum!

pictured overleaf

FOR THE MEATBALL PANINIS (SERVES 2)
2 small ciabatta loaves, or paninis
4–6 Mia's Meatballs, plus 4–6 tbsp of their sauce, both hot/reheated

Take each bread and cut it in half vertically. Pull out some of the soft crumb from the middle of each half and set aside.

Fill each panino with 2–3 hot meatballs and 2–3 tbsp of the amazing sauce. Take the pieces of bread you set aside and use them to seal the ends of each panino, so the filling doesn't leak out when you bite into it. Now you are ready to eat!

SLOW-COOKED VEAL SHANKS IN RED WINE AND PANCETTA SAUCE

OSSOBUCO

◆◆◆◆◆◆◆◆◆◆◆◆◆◆◆◆◆◆◆◆◆◆◆◆◆◆◆◆

This dish will definitely get a few ooohs and ahhhs. You will most probably have to order the cut of meat from your local butcher, but it is absolutely worth it. Whenever I make this recipe, whether it is for my family or for friends, it never disappoints. Remember to get everyone to spoon out the marrow when the meat is eaten – for me, that's the best bit.

SERVES 6

plain flour, to dust

6 veal shanks, about 1.5kg in total, each about 7cm thick

5 tbsp olive oil

1 large onion, finely chopped

2 large celery sticks, finely chopped

2 large carrots, finely chopped

100g pancetta, diced

3 thyme sprigs

2 tbsp tomato purée

100ml white wine

600ml warm chicken stock

2 tbsp runny honey

fine sea salt and freshly ground black pepper

Preheat the oven to 170°C/fan 150°C/Gas 3½.

Place some flour on a plate and season it with 1 tsp salt and ½ tsp pepper. Dip the veal shanks into the flour, ensuring the meat is well coated. Shake off the excess flour.

Pour the oil into a casserole dish and set over a medium heat. Gently place in the veal shanks and fry for 5 minutes on each side. Remove, place on a clean plate and set aside.

In the same casserole dish, fry the onion, celery and carrots for 2 minutes. Add the pancetta and fry it for a further 8 minutes, stirring occasionally. Put in the thyme and tomato purée and mix together with a wooden spoon.

Pour in the wine and simmer for 5 minutes, allowing the alcohol to evaporate. Pour over the stock and stir with a wooden spoon. Gently return the veal shanks to the casserole dish, cover with a lid and place in the preheated oven for 1 hour.

Remove the lid, gently stir the gravy, drizzle over the honey and cook without the lid for a further 30 minutes, allowing the sauce to thicken. Serve with buttery crushed potatoes and/or seasonal greens.

BEEF WELLINGTON WITH DUCK PÂTÉ

MANZO ALLA WELLINGTON CON PATÉ DI ANATRA

◆◆◆◆◆◆◆◆◆◆◆◆◆◆◆◆◆◆◆◆◆◆◆◆◆

This will be the easiest Wellington you will ever make, as we are cheating a bit by using shop-bought pâté and puff pastry, but the flavours will be just as good. There is something about serving up this dish to your guests that always gets a 'wow' and yet it's actually quite simple to put together. The best thing about it is that you can prepare it the night before and just put it into the oven when your guests arrive, allowing you to socialise with them rather than fuss about something cooking. You can substitute the duck pâté with mushroom pâté, if you prefer.

SERVES 4

800g middle-cut beef fillet, trimmed

4 tbsp brandy

3 tsp English mustard

200g duck pâté

10 slices of Parma ham

4 tbsp plain flour

500g ready-to-roll puff pastry

1 egg

fine sea salt and freshly ground
   black pepper

sea salt flakes

Season the beef with a pinch each of fine salt and pepper and place in a hot frying pan. Pour over the brandy and cook for 1 minute on each side and 30 seconds on each end, searing the beef all over. Remove from the pan, and, using a pastry brush, smother the beef with the mustard. Set aside, allowing to cool for 10 minutes.

Place the pâté on a plate, and, using a fork, remove and discard its jelly. Mash the rest into a smooth pulp. Spoon the pâté on top of the beef and squash down with your fingertips, ensuring it covers the whole top of the beef.

Put a sheet of cling film, about 40 x 35cm, on a work surface. Arrange the Parma ham at one end of the cling film, overlapping the slices slightly. Place the pâté-side of the beef upside down on top of the ham. Grab both sides of the cling film and roll away from you 2–3 times, creating a tight cylinder effect with the beef enclosed in the ham. Twist the ends of the cling film to seal and chill in the fridge for 45 minutes.

Sprinkle the flour on a clean dry work surface and roll out the pastry into a rectangular shape, large enough to envelop the beef with a little overlap, ensuring there is 3–4cm extra pastry at each end. Remove the cling film from the beef and place the meat in the centre of the pastry. Wrap the pastry tightly around the beef to enclose and press the ends firmly to seal.

Taking another large piece of cling film, wrap the Wellington tightly in the same way as before, twisting the ends again, and place in the fridge for 1 hour. This will ensure your beef Wellington is compact when cooking.

When ready to cook, take the beef Wellington out of the fridge and preheat the oven to 200°C/fan 180°C/Gas 6 for at least 15 minutes.

Remove the cling film, and, using the back of a knife, lightly score the top with diagonal lines. Beat the egg in a small bowl, and, using a pastry brush, brush the pastry with the egg. Season with sea salt flakes and a sprinkle of pepper.

Line a baking tray with baking parchment. Put the Wellington into the centre and bake for 45 minutes for medium-rare and 10 minutes longer for medium-well done. Remove from the oven and leave to rest for 10 minutes.

Slice into 4 equal portions (giving the ends to people who like their meat slightly more cooked), and serve with onion gravy, roast potatoes or mash and veg of your choice (I like cavolo nero). The ultimate Sunday lunch… followed by a sleep on the sofa.

pictured overleaf

KIDS ARE OUT

◆◆◆◆◆◆◆◆◆◆◆◆◆◆◆◆◆◆◆◆◆◆◆◆◆◆◆◆◆◆

I have called this chapter 'Kids Are Out' as many of the recipes here are meals that Jessica and I like to cook for each other when it is just the two of us. To be honest though, as the years have gone by, many of these dishes have become what we boys make when we're hanging out together while the girls go out and vice versa, so really they are for everyone and anyone. We all love so many of them that we also often double-up the quantities and eat them together as a family meal.

I think cooking with your children or your partner is so important, but for different reasons. Cooking with kids is amazing. It helps them establish a good relationship with food, and, when they are young, it can even help with their maths. It's also great fun, and, as they get older, it gives them a life skill they will always need and use. Cooking with your partner can be very romantic. It gives you something creative and fun to do together during your busy lives. Even if I am cooking and Jess is just sitting with me in the kitchen sipping a glass of wine, or helping me tidy up as I go, it's time we really cherish spending together.

I am a true believer that meal times can be a really special opportunity to spend quality time with your family, rather than a chore, but it does take everyone to get on board. No one wants to be the person abandoned alone in the kitchen, quietly getting the job done by themselves. So even if it's just once a week, give cooking together a try.

Jessica has made me promise to put a note from her in this section, so here it is: 'If you really can't find time to cook together, make sure you at least teach your partners how to make you the Chocolate Hazelnut Martini in this chapter, it is the next best thing!'

◆◆◆◆◆◆◆◆◆◆◆◆◆◆◆◆◆◆◆◆◆◆◆◆◆◆◆◆◆◆

PRAWN COCKTAIL WITH GARLIC CIABATTA

COCKTAIL DI GAMBERONI

◆◆◆◆◆◆◆◆◆◆◆◆◆◆◆◆◆◆◆◆◆◆◆◆◆

Some recipes have been around for a long time with good reason. This is one of those old-fashioned recipes, that, to me, is still massively worthy of being on any dining table, either for lunch or as a starter. It takes minutes to prepare and tastes amazing. Often, prawn cocktails on restaurant menus have been given a modern update, with lots of other ingredients added. Of course, those variations will taste great, but, to me, the prawns and sauce are the stars and the rest is just the chorus, so I've prepared it that way.

SERVES 2 AS A STARTER, OR LIGHT LUNCH

3 tbsp olive oil

3 garlic cloves, 2 finely sliced, 1 halved

12 large king prawns, heads, tails and shells removed

1 tbsp mayonnaise

½ tbsp tomato ketchup

½ tsp Tabasco sauce

½ tsp paprika

1 lemon

1 Little Gem lettuce, sliced

handful of rocket leaves (about 15g)

2 tbsp extra virgin olive oil

4 slices of ciabatta, about 1cm thick

fine sea salt and freshly ground black pepper

Put the regular olive oil and garlic slices into a medium frying pan and place over a high heat until the garlic starts to sizzle. Add the prawns with a pinch each of salt and pepper and fry for 1½ minutes, then turn them all over and fry for a further 1½ minutes. Remove with a slotted spoon and place on some kitchen paper to cool. Set aside.

Spoon the mayonnaise into a small bowl with the ketchup, Tabasco, paprika and the juice of half the lemon. Mix well.

Place the lettuce and rocket leaves in a medium bowl and season with a pinch each of salt and pepper and the extra virgin olive oil. Toss gently to combine.

Put your cooled prawns into the bowl of Marie Rose sauce and mix to completely coat the prawns in the sauce.

Place the ciabatta slices on a preheated griddle pan, or into a toaster, until toasted. Rub the halved clove of garlic on each slice.

Take 2 plates and divide the salad between them, ensuring the leaves create a bed for the prawns. Equally divide the prawns on top. Place 2 slices of garlic ciabatta bread on the side of each plate and garnish with a lemon quarter. Squeeze the lemon over the prawns and enjoy. Sometimes the old ways are the best ways!

SEAFOOD RISOTTO

RISOTTO AI FRUTTI DI MARE CON SCORZETTA DI LIMONE

◆◆◆◆◆◆◆◆◆◆◆◆◆◆◆◆◆◆◆◆◆◆◆◆◆◆◆

Taking Rocco to Naples was one of my all-time favourite experiences while we were filming the show that goes alongside this book, but making him my mother's seafood risotto while we were there was just so special: the icing on the cake. I have made this recipe countless times for the family over the years, but, somehow, cooking it on my home turf brought all of us closer to my parents… and that was a really wonderful feeling. Please try and get your seafood from a fishmonger, which will ensure that it is super-fresh. This recipe is from me to you from my mamma, with love.

SERVES 2

250g live clams

250g live mussels

80ml olive oil, plus more to serve

2 garlic cloves, finely sliced

1 tsp chilli flakes

300ml dry white wine

150g vialone nano risotto rice

150g raw prawns, shelled and deveined, the 4 nicest kept whole, the rest roughly chopped

800ml hot fish stock

handful of flat leaf parsley leaves

40g salted butter, chopped

finely grated zest of 1 unwaxed lemon

fine sea salt

Scrub the clams and mussels under cold running water. Rinse away the grit and remove barnacles with a small, sharp knife. Remove the 'beards' from the mussels by pulling the dark, stringy pieces away from the shells. Drop the clams from a height into a large bowl a few times, to help them expel their sand, then wash briefly in cold water for a couple of minutes. Check none of the clams are open or broken. Discard any open clams and mussels that do not shut when tapped firmly on the sink, or any with broken shells. Set aside in a colander.

Put 2 tbsp of the olive oil in a wide saucepan with a lid. Add half the garlic and allow to warm in the pan with the oil so it becomes fragrant, but the garlic doesn't burn. Add a pinch of the chilli flakes and fry for a few seconds, then add the clams, mussels and half the wine. Cover with a lid and leave to steam and open for 4–5 minutes. Pour the clams, mussels and their juices into a bowl and set aside.

In the same pan, heat another 2 tbsp of the oil and the remaining garlic and fry gently, along with another pinch of chilli flakes. Then add the rice and stir continuously for 2 minutes until the grains are coated and shiny. Pour in the remaining wine and stir until absorbed. Add the chopped prawns to cook gently.

When the wine has been absorbed, start adding the stock slowly, waiting until the liquid has been absorbed before adding the next bit, and stirring occasionally.

Meanwhile, pick half the meat from the clams and mussels and add to the risotto with some of their cooking liquid, although avoid adding the last bits, as they may be sandy.

Tear the parsley into small pieces and add to the risotto. After roughly 18 minutes the rice should be almost cooked and the stock nearly absorbed. Add the rest of the clams and mussels in their shells, stir to combine and then take off the heat.

Add the butter and stir, so the risotto becomes creamy. Leave to rest for 2 minutes while you heat a small frying pan over a high heat with the remaining olive oil. Add the 4 whole prawns, season with salt and fry for 1 minute on each side until just cooked and juicy, then remove from the heat. Add most of the lemon zest to the risotto and check the seasoning before serving on warmed plates, topped with the fried prawns, remaining lemon zest and a drizzle of olive oil.

pictured overleaf

PIZZA WITH BURRATA AND PARMA HAM

PIZZA CON BURRATA E PROSCIUTTO DI PARMA

◆◆◆◆◆◆◆◆◆◆◆◆◆◆◆◆◆◆◆◆◆◆◆◆◆◆◆◆◆◆

This has to be the quickest way to make a good pizza using a regular oven. There is nothing more satisfying than making your own pizza and it's a really nice thing to do as a couple, or with your kids. I have used burrata, which is a fantastic creamy mozzarella, but of course any mozzarella would work too. Pitted black olives are a nice extra flavour here, if you fancy.

MAKES 2

extra virgin olive oil

200g strong white bread flour, plus more to dust

½ tsp fast-action dried yeast

150ml tomato passata

2 x 125g burrata balls

10 basil leaves

8 slices of Parma ham

fine sea salt and freshly ground black pepper

Brush 2 medium-sized baking trays with olive oil.

Place the flour, yeast and ½ tsp salt into a large bowl, make a well in the centre and pour in 140ml warm water with 2 tbsp olive oil. Mix everything together using the handle of a wooden spoon, creating a wet dough.

Turn out the dough on to a well-floured surface and knead it with your hands for about 5 minutes until smooth and elastic. Shape the dough into 2 balls and place one in the centre of each of the oiled baking trays. Brush the top of the dough balls with a little oil and cover with cling film. Leave at room temperature to rest for 30 minutes.

Preheat the oven to 210°C/fan 190°C/Gas 6½.

Pour the passata into a small jug and stir in ½ tsp salt, a pinch of pepper and 2 tbsp olive oil. Set aside.

Once rested and still on the baking trays, use your hands to push each dough ball out from the centre, creating 2 round discs each about 25cm in diameter.

Equally spread the tomato mixture on top of the pizza bases. The best way to do this is by pouring the tomato mixture into the middle of the pizza bases and spreading it from the centre outwards, using the back of a tablespoon. Leave a 1cm border clear.

Bake in the middle of the oven for 13 minutes. Remove the trays from the oven, and, with your fingertips, equally break the burrata over the tomato mixture and scatter the basil leaves on top. Continue to bake for a final 2 minutes. Lay 4 slices of Parma ham on top of each pizza and serve immediately with a cold beer.

GRILLED SWORDFISH WITH SALSA VERDE

PESCE SPADA ALLA GRIGLIA CON SALSA VERDE

Luciano and I were in Scilla, in Calabria, and I took him on a special swordfish fishing boat called a *spadara*. The way they catch swordfish has stayed the same (or quite similar) for 2,000 years and a *spadara* has a 20m-tall mast, from which fishermen spot the swordfish and guide the boat. The men then try to harpoon the fish. There is something so much more respectful about catching fish this way, rather than by means of nets that catch and kill so many other species that are just thrown away. Cooking fish that has literally just come out of the sea is such a treat – very little interference is needed, allowing the fish to be the star of the show – so make sure your swordfish is as fresh as possible.

SERVES 2

2 x 200g swordfish fillet steaks

100ml extra virgin olive oil

large handful of flat leaf parsley leaves

2 garlic cloves

1 tbsp capers in brine, drained

4 anchovies in oil

1 tbsp pitted green olives

small handful of basil leaves

juice of 1 lemon

80g frisee lettuce

fine sea salt and freshly ground
   black pepper

Place a griddle pan over a high heat.

Drizzle the fish with 1 tbsp of the olive oil and rub it all over both sides with a pinch of salt. When the griddle is smoking hot, gently place in the fish and cook for 2 minutes on each side. When grilled, place on a plate to rest.

For the salsa verde, start by chopping the parsley relatively finely. Chop the garlic next to the parsley on the board and then combine them and chop together. On top, add the capers and anchovies and continue to chop all together. Then add the olives and lastly the basil and continue to chop until everything is relatively finely chopped.

Transfer to a bowl and mix with the remaining olive oil, the lemon juice and a bit of pepper to make a lovely sauce. Check the seasoning and adjust if necessary.

Serve each swordfish steak on a plate topped with a handful of the crunchy frisee, then dress with the delicious salsa verde. Use any leftover salsa verde on any grilled meat or seafood; it will keep well in the fridge for 48 hours.

CHICKEN IN MARSALA SAUCE

POLLO AL MARSALA

◆◆◆◆◆◆◆◆◆◆◆◆◆◆◆◆◆◆◆◆◆◆◆◆◆

I could not write a D'Acampo family cookbook without this recipe in it. This is Jessica's all-time-favourite meal. It is one of the first dinners I ever cooked for her and is still received with huge smiles after twenty-six years, the biggest of which was when I made it for her on the show and proceeded to ask her to remarry me. I'm not sure what she was most excited about, me or the dish. I have accompanied it with salad, but, if it was up to her, she would have it with my Gino's Roast Potatoes or Spicy Brussels Sprouts (see pages 90 and 91).

SERVES 2

2 large chicken breasts

4 tbsp plain flour

50g salted butter

6 tbsp extra virgin olive oil

125ml Marsala

150ml double cream

½ tsp paprika

70g rocket leaves

1 small radicchio, roughly shredded

1 tbsp white wine vinegar

fine sea salt and freshly ground
    black pepper

Place a chicken breast on a chopping board and put one hand on top of it to keep it steady. Using a sharp knife, slice horizontally into the thickest part of the breast (keeping the chicken breasts whole); you are just trying to make the chicken breasts of a consistent thickness throughout. Place the flour on a plate and then lay each piece of chicken into it. Season generously on one side with salt and pepper and pat the seasoning into the flesh. Turn the chicken over and repeat on the other side, then dust off any excess flour so it is lightly coated, then transfer to another plate.

Put the butter into a cold frying pan and allow to melt gently as it comes up to a medium heat. When the butter has melted, add 3 tbsp of the olive oil to stop it from burning, then, when it starts to sizzle gently, lay in the chicken. Fry the chicken for 6 minutes on one side, then turn when golden brown. Fry for another 5 minutes before draining off any excess fat.

Add the Marsala to the pan and flambé if you can – tipping the pan away from you and lighting the liquid carefully with a long match – allowing it to boil and burn off the alcohol. Then add the cream and bring to a simmer before removing the chicken from the pan to rest.

Let the sauce simmer gently to thicken, then finish by adding the paprika and seasoning with salt and pepper. In a bowl, dress the rocket and radicchio with the remaining 3 tbsp of olive oil, the vinegar, salt and pepper. Serve the chicken with the sauce drizzled on top and the salad on the side.

SPAGHETTI WITH JUICY CLAMS AND BOTTARGA

SPAGHETTI ALLE VONGOLE E BOTTARGA

◆◆◆◆◆◆◆◆◆◆◆◆◆◆◆◆◆◆◆◆◆◆◆◆

This is Mia's favourite pasta dish. It was so much fun making it with her in Porto Cervo in Sardinia and seeing how much she loved the whole experience of filming and cooking with me. I have made this recipe a couple of times since filming the show and she always reminisces about the day we had together. Food = memories = love. This recipe will always be yours, my princess.

SERVES 2

120ml extra virgin olive oil

2 garlic cloves, roughly chopped

1–2 red chillies, sliced

500g live clams

100ml dry white wine, ideally vermentino

250g dried spaghetti

100g cherry tomatoes, roughly chopped

handful of flat leaf parsley leaves, roughly chopped

10g bottarga from a large piece, freshly grated

fine sea salt

Bring a large saucepan of water to the boil. Meanwhile, put half the olive oil into a saucepan and place over a medium heat. Add the garlic and chilli(es) and fry gently for 1 minute so the oil takes on all the flavours and becomes fragrant. Remove from the heat while you clean the clams.

Drop the clams from a height into a large bowl a few times, to help them expel their sand, then wash briefly in cold water for a couple of minutes. Check none of the clams are open or broken, and, if they are, discard them. Return the pan with the garlic to the heat, and, when just sizzling, add the clams along with the white wine, then clamp a tight lid on and leave to steam for 4–5 minutes over a medium heat.

Meanwhile, salt the boiling water well and add the spaghetti, making sure it is completely submerged.

When all the clams have opened, remove the lid. Check for any that have remained closed and discard those. Add the tomatoes and parsley and simmer with the clams for a minute, then remove from the heat. Carefully separate the meat from about half the clam shells, leaving the meat in the sauce and discarding the empty shells. When the spaghetti is perfectly al dente (usually 1 minute less than instructed on the packet), return the sauce to the heat and use tongs to transfer the pasta straight into the pan of sauce.

Toss the pasta with the sauce for a minute or so, drizzling in the remaining olive oil. Serve immediately with grated bottarga on top.

RIGATONI IN CREAMY SAUCE WITH FRIED COURGETTE AND PEAS

RIGATONI CON ZUCCHINE FRITTE E PISELLI

✦✦✦✦✦✦✦✦✦✦✦✦✦✦✦✦✦✦✦✦✦✦✦✦✦

This is the ultimate fast food in the D'Acampo household. We always have these ingredients in our cupboards or fridge, it takes no time to make and is absolutely delicious. All of us love this for lunch or dinner, and, if the kids are out and we have had enough of cooking for everyone all week, Jess and I often turn to this meal. You can use tortiglioni (larger pasta tubes) instead of rigatoni if you prefer, and, if you buy Italian products, you can use a carton of Panna Chef cream sauce instead of double cream.

SERVES 2

1 large courgette, about 300g

6 tbsp extra virgin olive oil

100g frozen peas, defrosted

200ml double cream

250g dried rigatoni pasta

10 cherry tomatoes, quartered

30g finely grated Parmesan cheese

fine sea salt and freshly ground
   black pepper

Fill a large saucepan with 4 litres of water, add 1 tbsp salt and bring to the boil over a high heat.

Meanwhile, discard 1cm from the top and bottom of the courgette and cut the rest into 5mm cubes.

Pour the olive oil into a large frying pan and place over a high heat. Add the courgette, sprinkle over ½ tsp salt and ½ tsp pepper and fry for 10 minutes, stirring occasionally with a wooden spoon. Add the peas, stir and cook for a further 2 minutes. Reduce the heat to medium, pour in the cream, stir and cook for 1 minute. Turn off the heat and set aside.

Cook the pasta in the boiling water until al dente. To get the al dente perfect bite, cook the pasta for 1 minute less than instructed on the packet and always cook it with the lid off. Stir every minute or so.

Once the pasta is cooked, drain well and tip back in the same saucepan, off the heat. Pour over the creamy courgette and pea sauce. Add the tomatoes and half the Parmesan and mix all together for 10 seconds.

Serve immediately in warmed plates or bowls, with the remaining Parmesan sprinkled on top.

SPICY MUSSELS AND CLAMS WITH GARLIC AND WHITE WINE

SAUTÉ DI COZZE E VONGOLE PICCANTINO

◆◆◆◆◆◆◆◆◆◆◆◆◆◆◆◆◆◆◆◆◆◆◆◆◆

I wasn't sure what chapter to put this in, as it is amazing for a Sunday Special, low-calorie enough to go in Lighter, fast enough to work in the Quick chapter and also a fantastic One Pot wonder! I put it into this chapter in the end, as I like the idea of making a seafood meal just for two, and enjoying it close together. *Cozze* and *vongole* are amazing together and both remind me so much of Italy. I hope this recipe takes you on the same journey.

SERVES 2

1kg live mussels

300g live clams

3 tbsp extra virgin olive oil

3 garlic cloves, sliced

½ tsp chilli flakes

150ml dry white wine

20 cherry tomatoes, halved

3 tbsp roughly chopped flat leaf parsley leaves

fine sea salt and freshly ground black pepper

Scrub the mussels and clams under cold running water. Rinse away the grit and remove barnacles with a small, sharp knife. Remove the 'beards' from the mussels by pulling the dark, stringy pieces away from the shells. Discard any open mussels or clams that do not shut when tapped firmly on the sink, or any with broken shells. Drop the clams from a height into a large bowl a few times, to help them expel their sand, then wash briefly in cold water for a couple of minutes. Check none of the clams are open or broken, and, if they are, discard them. Set aside in a colander.

Pour the olive oil into a large saucepan and place over a high heat. Add the garlic and chilli, and, as soon as the garlic starts to sizzle, follow with the mussels and clams. Stir all together with a wooden spoon and cook for 2 minutes. Pour over the wine and continue to cook for a further 3 minutes, allowing for all the alcohol to evaporate. Stir occasionally.

Cover the saucepan with a tight-fitting lid and continue to cook for 3 minutes, until the mussels and clams start to open.

Remove the lid, add the cherry tomatoes, parsley, 1 tsp salt and 1 tsp pepper, stir all together and cook for a final 5 minutes, again stirring occasionally. Discard any mussels or clams that remain closed.

Ladle into a large warmed bowl so 2 people can just tuck in and eat together, and serve immediately with warm crusty bread for dunky-dunky.

GRILLED CHICKEN IN CREAMY MUSHROOM SAUCE WITH THYME AND GARLIC

PETTI DI POLLO CON FUNGHI CREMOSI AL TIMO E AGLIO

Although nowadays most ingredients can be bought all year round, I am still a strong believer that we should always try to buy produce in season whenever we can, and this is the perfect autumn dish to celebrate mushrooms. If you prefer, you can substitute the thyme for rosemary, and, if you are vegetarian, this sauce works really well with rice, polenta or tofu. You can also substitute the pecorino cheese for Parmesan, if you prefer.

SERVES 2

50g salted butter

1 tbsp chopped thyme leaves

3 tbsp olive oil, plus more for the chicken

400g mixed mushrooms, roughly sliced

2 garlic cloves, finely sliced

50ml dry white wine

250ml double cream

10 cherry tomatoes, halved

2 large skinless chicken breast fillets, about 250g each

2 tbsp finely grated pecorino cheese (about 25g)

fine sea salt and freshly ground black pepper

Place a large frying pan or a wok over a high heat and melt the butter, adding the thyme with the 3 tbsp olive oil. Now add the mushrooms with 1 tsp salt and fry for 5 minutes, stirring occasionally with a wooden spoon. Add the garlic and continue to fry for a further 5 minutes.

Pour over the wine and bring to the boil for 2 minutes. Reduce the heat to medium and stir in the cream with the cherry tomatoes and ½ tsp pepper. Cook for a further 5 minutes, stirring occasionally.

Meanwhile, preheat a griddle pan over a high heat for 5 minutes.

Place a chicken breast on a chopping board and put one hand on top of it to keep it steady. Slice it in half horizontally, then repeat with the other, to create 4 thin chicken breasts. Brush with olive oil on both sides and place in the hot griddle pan. (You may need to do this in 2 batches, depending on the size of your pan or the chicken.) Cook for 4 minutes on each side.

Place 2 slices of grilled chicken on each of 2 warmed plates, spoon over the creamy garlic mushrooms and sprinkle 1 tbsp grated pecorino cheese on each dish.

This is fantastic with a chilled glass of Italian white wine.

RACK OF LAMB WITH PEAS AND SMOKED PANCETTA

COSTOLETTE DI AGNELLO CON PISELLI E PANCETTA AFFUMICATA

◆◆◆◆◆◆◆◆◆◆◆◆◆◆◆◆◆◆◆◆◆◆◆◆◆

This used to be my 'guilty' recipe that I'd make for my boys. Whenever Jessica and I went out together and left them at home, they hated it, so I always made them this meal as compensation. When I told them what I was cooking them for dinner before we left, the moaning stopped! Still to this day they often ask me to make it for them, and now we use the same tactic on Mia, too (even though chocolate works better for her at the moment). This dish really looks impressive plated, so it's also perfect for dinner guests, just scale up the ingredients accordingly.

SERVES 2

100g smoked pancetta, diced

150g frozen peas, defrosted

4 tbsp olive oil

6 large thyme sprigs

4 large garlic cloves, unpeeled, halved lengthways

2 baby racks of lamb, about 250g each, bones trimmed

1 tbsp good-quality mint sauce, plus 2 tsp to serve

½ tbsp runny honey

knob of salted butter

fine sea salt and freshly ground black pepper

sea salt flakes

Place a medium frying pan over a medium heat, add the pancetta and fry for 5 minutes, stirring occasionally with a wooden spoon. Add the peas with a pinch each of fine salt and pepper and stir. Pour in 5 tbsp water, mix well and cook for 5 minutes. Turn off the heat and set aside.

Preheat the oven to 200°C/fan 180°C/Gas 6.

Pour the olive oil into an ovenproof frying pan and add the thyme and garlic. Set over a medium heat, and, as soon as they start to sizzle, place in the lamb, fat-side down. Fry for 5 minutes. Sprinkle over a pinch each of fine salt and pepper, and, using tongs, stand the racks on their ends to fry on each end for 1 minute. Lay them back down, now fat-side up, and sprinkle over another pinch each of fine salt and pepper.

Remove from the heat and place in the middle of the preheated oven. Roast for 20 minutes for medium-rare meat.

Meanwhile, put the 1 tbsp of mint sauce into a small bowl, add the honey and mix well. Set aside.

When the lamb is ready, take it out of the oven and place on a chopping board. Brush the racks all over with the mint and honey glaze, cover with foil and allow to rest for 5 minutes. As the meat is resting, add the knob of butter to the peas and pancetta and reheat them over a high heat for 5 minutes. Slice the lamb racks between the bones, creating lamb cutlets, if you like.

Equally portion out the peas and pancetta between 2 warmed plates to create a bed and gently lay the lamb on top. Drizzle over the oil from the pan, sprinkle over a pinch of sea salt flakes and place 1 tsp of mint sauce on the side of each plate. Serve with my Simple Spicy Spinach with Garlic and Olive Oil (see page 89), and a cold glass of red wine: we love any red wine chilled and often prefer it that way, especially during the hotter months.

pictured overleaf

ROCCO'S ULTIMATE FILLET STEAK SANDWICH

IL PANINO DI ROCCO

◆◆◆◆◆◆◆◆◆◆◆◆◆◆◆◆◆◆◆◆◆◆◆◆◆◆◆◆◆

I have to dedicate this recipe to my son Rocco. This is our go-to whenever we want to watch a film or sport together. It is the only time I allow food on the sofa, and, I must admit, it makes it so much more special somehow. It really takes no time at all to make, but the ingredients together are a match made in heaven… and so is our precious time together. You can substitute the bacon for sliced pancetta if you prefer, and I suggest having lots of tissues to hand, as eating this without egg running down your fingers is a real challenge!

SERVES 2

2 ciabatta loaves or baguettes, each about 20cm long

2 tsp English mustard

2 tbsp mayonnaise

2 handfuls of rocket leaves, or any salad of your choice

400g fillet steak, cut into 6 slices about 1cm thick

3 tbsp olive oil

4 bacon rashers

4 large eggs

fine sea salt and freshly ground black pepper

Cut the bread in half lengthways and remove any excess dough, creating space for the filling (you can blitz this up to make breadcrumbs for another recipe, no need to waste it). Spread 1 tsp of mustard inside each loaf: ½ tsp on the top and ½ tsp on the bottom. Now spread 1 tbsp of mayonnaise inside each loaf: again ½ tbsp on the top and ½ tbsp on the bottom. Place a handful of leaves across the bottom half of each loaf and set aside.

Press each fillet steak slice down on a chopping board with your palm, creating an oval shape. Pour the olive oil into a frying pan and place over a medium heat. Add the bacon and fry for 4 minutes, then turn over and fry for a further 2 minutes. Remove from the pan and rest on a plate. Gently place the fillet steaks into the same hot frying pan and fry them for 1 minute on each side. Season with a pinch each of salt and pepper and rest on a plate with the bacon. Finally, crack the eggs into the same hot oiled pan and fry to your preferred doneness; I like mine runny.

Take the bread and place the bacon on top of the leaves. Lay the steak on top of the bacon and then top with the fried eggs. Seriously, this is the steak sandwich at its best.

CHOCOLATE HAZELNUT MARTINI

MARTINI CON CREMA DI NOCCIOLE E CIOCCOLATO

◆◆◆◆◆◆◆◆◆◆◆◆◆◆◆◆◆◆◆◆◆◆◆◆◆

This is a fantastic alternative to any dessert, quick to make, extremely satisfying, and, most importantly… delicious. If you prefer, you can substitute the Cointreau with Amaretto, and also decorate the rim of the glasses with bitter cocoa powder. My wife Jessica and I drink this at least once a week and that could be the secret to our happy marriage.

SERVES 2

300ml single cream

3 tbsp chocolate-hazelnut spread (such as Nutella), about 90g

about 10 ice cubes

4 tbsp vodka

4 tbsp Cointreau

Pour the cream into a small saucepan and place it over a low heat. Stir in the chocolate-hazelnut spread and stir with a whisk all together, making sure that the cream does not reach boiling point. Set aside for 20 minutes, allowing the chocolate cream to cool down, stirring occasionally.

Place the ice in a cocktail shaker to come three-quarters of the way up and pour over the vodka and Cointreau. Pour the cooled chocolate-cream mix into the shaker, close with the lid and shake for 15 seconds.

Strain the drink into 2 martini glasses, leaving the ice behind, and serve immediately. Heaven in a glass!

pictured overleaf

ORANGE AND GRAND MARNIER BISCUITS

ARANCETTI

◆◆◆◆◆◆◆◆◆◆◆◆◆◆◆◆◆◆◆◆◆◆◆◆◆◆◆

Whenever my wife and I are in the mood to watch a film together and I need to convince her to watch yet another Marvel film, or one of the *Godfather* collections, I bribe her with these biscuits and a glass of red wine. It's our midnight feast and we love it. For a stronger orange liqueur flavour, you can use Cointreau, or, if you prefer, you can substitute the orange zest with the zest of three unwaxed lemons and the orange liqueur with limoncello.

MAKES ABOUT 48

1 tbsp salted butter, for the tray

4 egg whites

350g caster sugar

finely grated zest of 2 large oranges
   (ideally unwaxed, if possible)

350g ground almonds

3 tbsp Grand Marnier

icing sugar, to dust

Preheat the oven to 180°C/fan 160°C/Gas 4.

Line a large baking tray with greaseproof paper and lightly butter it with the 1 tbsp butter.

Place the egg whites in a large, clean, dry bowl and whisk until stiff and firm. Add the sugar and whisk to combine for about 30 seconds. Using a spatula, gently fold in the orange zest and almonds. Pour in the orange liqueur and fold carefully to make a smooth, thick paste, ensuring that all the ingredients are combined.

Using a teaspoon, place small heaps of the mixture on to the prepared tray, spaced about 3cm apart to allow for expansion during cooking. (You will need to bake them in 2 batches.)

Bake in the middle of the oven for 14 minutes, until light golden brown.

Enjoy warm, or dry the biscuits on a wire rack until firm. Dust with a little icing sugar on top: the perfect midnight feast!

pictured overleaf

DESSERTS

◆◆◆◆◆◆◆◆◆◆◆◆◆◆◆◆◆◆◆◆◆◆◆◆◆◆

I could probably fill an entire book with dessert recipes. My wife and kids all have a huge sweet tooth, and so do I, but we all love different things. Luciano likes ice creams, sorbets and fruit concoctions, whereas Rocco is a soufflé and cake kind of guy. Mia loves anything chocolate, while Jessica will always go for citrus flavours or tarts and she loves a cheesecake. As for me, I love an Italian tiramisù or semifreddo as well as traditional British pies or puddings with custard.

You see, I have covered all types of desserts with just my family's favourites. It was actually quite difficult to choose what to put in this chapter, as everyone at home seemed to have an opinion. Honestly, if it was up to Mia and Rocco, every recipe would have contained chocolate!

We love nothing more than enjoying a dessert together after dinner. I'd like to say that it was only on special occasions, but I'd be lying and I could never get away with that. One of the kids will always ask the 'What's for dessert?' question, most times even before the main meal has been served.

When the boys are studying for important exams, I always make them something sweet in the afternoon as a special treat or pick-me-up. The chocolate cake in this chapter is always received with huge smiles.

I think that we will please most people with the final recipes we picked. Many are really simple and quick to cook, and the ice creams, especially, are fantastic to make with younger kids. All of the desserts are great to serve up on a week day but are also impressive enough for dinner parties. I hope your family enjoys them as much as we do!

◆◆◆◆◆◆◆◆◆◆◆◆◆◆◆◆◆◆◆◆◆◆◆◆◆

ORANGE AND PISTACHIO TIRAMISÙ

TIRAMISÙ ALL'ARANCIA E PISTACCHI

◆◆◆◆◆◆◆◆◆◆◆◆◆◆◆◆◆◆◆◆◆◆◆◆◆◆◆◆◆

There is no denying that a traditional tiramisù enriched with coffee and Amaretto liqueur (see overleaf) will always be the ultimate Italian dessert, but so many people don't really like coffee, so I have to come up with other versions. Over the years I have created a chocolate tiramisù for the kids, lemon tiramisù for my in-laws… and now I think I have hit the jackpot with this orange version, as both kids and adults love it. Tiramisù is always a winner to make for dinner parties, as you can prepare it in the morning or even the night before and serve when you're all ready for it.

SERVES 6

4 eggs, separated

100g caster sugar

500g mascarpone cheese

2 oranges (ideally unwaxed, if possible)

4 tbsp Cointreau

12 Savoiardi biscuits

3 tbsp chopped pistachio nuts

Place the egg whites in a large clean bowl with 50g of the sugar and whisk with an electric whisk until firm peaks form.

Put the egg yolks and remaining 50g sugar into a separate large clean bowl and beat with the electric whisk for about 3 minutes until thick and pale. Add the mascarpone and whisk to combine. Grate over the zest of both oranges, and, using a spatula, gently fold all together. Now fold the egg whites into the mascarpone mixture, gently, so you don't lose the air bubbles and volume.

Pour 50ml cold water into a ceramic or glass tray and stir in the juice from the oranges with the Cointreau.

Place 2 tbsp of the mascarpone mix in each of 6 glasses (not heaped tablespoons, or you won't have enough).

Dip a biscuit into the orange water for just 2 seconds, cut in half and place on top of the orange mascarpone mixture, sugar-side up. (Do not dip the biscuits for longer otherwise they will turn soggy.) Do this for all 6 glasses.

Spread 2 more tbsp of the mascarpone mixture on top. Place the remaining biscuits (1 for each glass), again dipped in the orange water and halved, on top, sugar-side up. Finally, spread the remaining mascarpone cream on top, or use a piping bag, if you're feeling fancy. Cover with cling film and refrigerate for at least 4 hours.

Remove the cling film from the glasses and sprinkle ½ tbsp chopped pistachio nuts on top of each tiramisù.

JESS'S TIRAMISÙ

IL TIRAMISÙ DI JESSICA

◆◆◆◆◆◆◆◆◆◆◆◆◆◆◆◆◆◆◆◆◆◆◆◆◆

This was the first dessert I ever taught Jessica how to make. It's actually a traditional Italian tiramisù, but, because she has mastered it so well, and because whenever we have a dinner party or the kids fancy it, we ask her to make it, I had to name it Jess's Tiramisù. I have also created an alternative recipe for an orangey tiramisù if you fancy something a bit different (see page 216).

SERVES 8

200ml cold strong black coffee, preferably espresso

200ml Amaretto liqueur

5 eggs, separated

200ml double cream

6 tbsp caster sugar

500g mascarpone cheese

36 Savoiardi biscuits

cocoa powder, to dust

Pour the coffee and 100ml of the Amaretto into a small glass dish, stir and set aside.

Place the egg whites in a large bowl and whisk until firm peaks form. Pour the double cream into a medium bowl and whisk until soft peaks form. Set both bowls aside.

Put the egg yolks and sugar in a large bowl and whisk for about 4 minutes until thick and pale. (If you do the whisking in this order, there is no need to wash the whisk in between.) Add the mascarpone and beat thoroughly. Pour the remaining 100ml of Amaretto into the egg yolks, then fold in the cream.

Spoon half the egg whites into the mascarpone cream and gently fold in. Add the remaining egg whites and again gently fold in so you don't lose the air bubbles or volume. Set aside.

Dip 18 biscuits into the coffee mixture for just 2 seconds and use them to cover the base of a ceramic dish, about 30 x 20cm and at least 7cm tall, arranging them sugar-side up. (Do not dip the biscuits for longer or they will turn soggy.)

Spread half the mascarpone over the biscuits, then dip the remaining 18 biscuits in the coffee – again, for just 2 seconds – and add them, sugar-side up, to form another layer. Spread the remaining mascarpone on top.

Cover with cling film and refrigerate for at least 3 hours.

Just before serving (not before, or the cocoa powder will go bitter), remove the cling film and dust with cocoa powder.

IRISH CREAM PANNA COTTA WITH CHOCOLATE COFFEE BEANS

PANNA COTTA ALLA CREMA IRLANDESE

◆◆◆◆◆◆◆◆◆◆◆◆◆◆◆◆◆◆◆◆◆◆◆◆◆◆◆◆◆◆◆◆

I created this recipe especially for my mother, Alba. She absolutely loved Irish cream liqueur. Growing up, she would often whip up a traditional vanilla panna cotta for us all on a weekend as a special treat, but, as soon as she tried this recipe, it became her signature dish, not mine. If you prefer it the traditional way, substitute the liqueur for 100ml more milk and add a vanilla pod and its seeds when cooking the cream… but I'm pretty sure, once you try this dish, you will never go back! You will need four 175ml moulds, or you can use ramekins or even cleaned-out yogurt pots, if you like.

SERVES 4

100ml whole milk

300ml double cream

100ml Irish cream liqueur

50g caster sugar

2 gelatine leaves, or enough to set 400ml of liquid (check the instructions on the packet)

cocoa powder, to dust (optional)

8 chocolate-coated coffee beans

Pour the milk, cream, liqueur and sugar into a small saucepan and warm gently over a low heat, stirring continuously with a wooden spoon until the sugar dissolves and the cream starts to lightly bubble at the sides of the saucepan, about 6 minutes. Do not boil the milk. Remove from the heat and set aside.

Meanwhile, place the gelatine leaves in a bowl of cold water for 5 minutes. Squeeze them dry, then stir the gelatine leaves into the cream mixture until completely dissolved.

Divide the mixture between 4 x 175ml moulds, cover with cling film and refrigerate for at least 5 hours.

To serve, dust 4 plates with a little cocoa powder, or use a dark plate so the panna cotta will stand out. Dip the moulds into warm water for 20 seconds (make sure you don't get any of the water in the panna cottas), then carefully turn out on to the prepared plates. Place 2 chocolate-coated coffee beans on top of each and serve.

FROZEN BERRY ICE CREAM

GELATO ALLE BACCHE

◆◆◆◆◆◆◆◆◆◆◆◆◆◆◆◆◆◆◆◆◆◆◆◆◆◆

I have made frozen berry ice cream many times, but, after the success of my Ultimate Chocolate Chip Ice Cream challenge (see page 226), I wanted to try a similar method using frozen fruits… and it worked fantastically! You can substitute the condensed milk for 200g natural yogurt if you prefer a healthier option. If you decide to use yogurt, add six tablespoons of honey too, or the ice cream might taste a bit sour.

SERVES 8

400ml double cream
500g frozen mixed berries
400g can of condensed milk

Pour the cream into a large bowl, and, using an electric whisk, whip it into stiff peaks. Set aside.

Using a blender, mix the frozen berries and condensed milk together, creating a thick, creamy texture.

Pour the berry mixture into the cream, and, using a spatula, fold the ingredients together.

Pour the berry ice cream into a freezable plastic container that has a lid, cover with the lid and place in the freezer for 2 hours. Remove, stir with a fork and return to the freezer for a further 4 hours. If you are going to be leaving the ice cream in the freezer for a few days, always take it out to soften for 10 minutes before serving.

Scoop into bowls and enjoy.

COFFEE AND AMARETTO SEMIFREDDO

SEMIFREDDO AL CAFFÈ E AMARETTO

◆◆◆◆◆◆◆◆◆◆◆◆◆◆◆◆◆◆◆◆◆◆◆◆◆

Amaretto and coffee are a match made in heaven and I absolutely love the combination of flavours. I am also a huge fan of drinking an espresso after most meals, so, for me, this dessert is one of my absolute favourites. Ice cream can be too cold sometimes and mousses can be too sweet or heavy after certain dishes, so having these flavours in a texture that is something in between is perfect. You can store this in the freezer for up to six weeks, but I doubt it will last that long!

SERVES 6

300ml double cream

4 large eggs, separated

1 tbsp instant coffee granules

1 tbsp Amaretto

100g caster sugar

100g crunchy (not soft) amaretti biscuits, plus more to decorate

Line a 1kg loaf tin with cling film, making sure you have at least 10cm extra on each long side, so you can cover the top of the semifreddo.

Pour the cream into a medium bowl and set aside. Put the egg whites into a separate medium bowl and set aside.

Put the egg yolks into a large bowl. Stir in the coffee, the Amaretto and the sugar until the coffee granules dissolve.

Whisk the egg whites with an electric whisk until stiff peaks form. Whisk the coffee mixture until thick and creamy. Whip the cream until medium peaks form. If you do the whisking in this order, you will not need to clean your whisk in between!

Using a spatula, fold the cream into the coffee mixture. When combined, add the egg whites and fold them in gently, trying not to lose volume. Finally, taking 4–5 amaretti biscuits at a time, crush them in your hands, creating small and large pieces, and put these into the coffee cream mixture. Again, fold the ingredients all together.

Slowly pour the coffee cream mixture into the prepared loaf tin, cover the top with the overlapping cling film and put into the freezer for at least 6 hours, or ideally overnight.

When ready to serve, peel the cling film off the top and tip out on to a serving plate. Remove the cling film completely and place amaretti biscuits on top for decoration.

Cut into slices and enjoy.

ULTIMATE CHOCOLATE CHIP ICE CREAM

GELATO CON SCHEGGE DI CIOCCOLATO

◆◆◆◆◆◆◆◆◆◆◆◆◆◆◆◆◆◆◆◆◆◆◆◆◆

My son Rocco is always giving me cookery challenges and this amazing recipe came about on one of those occasions. He asked me why we don't have an ice-cream maker and I simply replied: we don't need one. He then challenged me to make a chocolate ice cream in less than ten minutes. I kind of cheated, as, although the prep time *is* less than ten minutes, you obviously have to leave it in the freezer for at least five hours… but let's not tell him that! This is a great recipe to make with your children as it's all done in one bowl: no mess and it's quick, too. You can mix up the chocolate chips if you like, using 100g of milk chocolate and 50g of either dark or white chocolate. I've even added leftover brownie cubes and marshmallows, too.

SERVES 8

500ml double cream

50g cocoa powder (try and get 100% cocoa if you can)

150g milk chocolate chips (or see recipe introduction)

400g can of condensed milk

Pour the cream into a large bowl, and, using an electric whisk, whip it into stiff peaks.

Add the cocoa powder, chocolate chips and condensed milk. Using a spatula, gently fold all the ingredients together until fully combined.

Pour the chocolate mixture into a freezable plastic container that has a lid, cover with the lid and place in the freezer for at least 5 hours to set. If you are going to be leaving the ice cream in the freezer for a few days, always take it out to soften for 10 minutes before serving.

I could suggest that you serve this in fancy glasses like we did for this photo, but, to be honest, in our house, it usually remains in the plastic container and we all crowd round with 5 spoons. Enjoy x

MANGO AND VODKA SORBET

SORBETTO CON MANGO E VODKA

◆◆◆◆◆◆◆◆◆◆◆◆◆◆◆◆◆◆◆◆◆◆◆◆◆◆◆◆◆

Sorbets have to be one of the easiest recipes to make. You take your chosen fruit – I have used mango in this recipe, but pineapple and mixed berries are also great – blitz in a food processor with the other ingredients and freeze. All done in five minutes. It is a fantastic dessert if you are trying to be healthy, and no one will even notice. It has a really refreshing flavour, which is great not only on hot summer days, but also after a heavy meal.

SERVES 6

500g frozen mango cubes
100ml vodka
3 tbsp runny honey

Place all the ingredients in a food processor with 300ml cold water and blitz until you create a thick creamy texture. You may have to manually stir it a couple of times to release any mango chunks from the blades.

Pour into a plastic freezable container, put the lid on top and freeze for 4 hours. If leaving the sorbet in the freezer for a few days, always take it out for 10 minutes before serving.

When ready to serve, scoop into bowls and enjoy.

D'ACAMPO CHRISTMAS MESS

IL DOLCE DI NATALE SCOMPOSTO DEI D'ACAMPO

◆◆◆◆◆◆◆◆◆◆◆◆◆◆◆◆◆◆◆◆◆◆◆◆◆◆◆◆◆

I concocted this cream-free version of an Eton mess, to give a more citrusy, fresh and less heavy taste, for a really light dessert that doesn't compromise on flavour. Perfect after any heavy meal. Being abroad for most Christmases, I have used strawberries, but of course always try to use the seasonal fruits that are available in your part of the world: anything works, and even frozen berries are fantastic.

SERVES 4–6

350g pitted cherries

350g strawberries, hulled and halved, or see recipe introduction

75g crunchy amaretti biscuits, crushed

50g mini meringues

40g toasted flaked almonds

40g crushed pistachio nuts

juice of 1 lemon

1 tsp sugar

200g dark chocolate, 70% cocoa solids, roughly chopped

In a bowl, gently mix the fruit with a few each of the crushed amaretti, meringues, toasted almonds and pistachios (save the rest for topping the dish when you serve it), then gently mix through all the lemon juice and sugar. Leave to marinate for 15 minutes.

Melt the chocolate gently in the microwave, or place in a heatproof bowl and melt over a small saucepan of simmering water (don't let the bowl touch the water).

When ready to serve, divide the fruit between serving bowls and top with the remaining crushed amaretti, meringues and nuts, then drizzle with the melted chocolate.

Serve immediately.

FERRERO ROCHER CHOCOLATE CAKE

TORTA AL FERRERO ROCHER

◆◆◆◆◆◆◆◆◆◆◆◆◆◆◆◆◆◆◆◆◆◆◆◆

You will never be in my house or even in my car without a Ferrero Rocher being available. This amazing ball of perfection – to the D'Acampo family – is like a cup of tea for most of us in the UK: essential on a daily basis. I created this recipe originally to make cupcakes with my daughter Mia, but have turned it into the ultimate cake, which can be eaten as a dessert or served at a tea party. To be honest, we have all had a slice for breakfast, too. No judgement from the D'Acampos if you decide to do the same!

SERVES 8

170g unsalted butter, at room temperature, plus more for the tin

16 Ferrero Rocher, crushed, plus 3 more to serve

250g caster sugar

4 large eggs

200g natural yogurt

230g self-raising flour, sifted

FOR THE TOPPING

150g dark chocolate, 70% cocoa solids, broken into small pieces

150ml double cream

4 tbsp crushed hazelnuts (about 40g)

Preheat the oven to 170°C/fan 150°C/Gas 3½ and butter a 22cm diameter, non-stick springform cake tin.

Take off the wrappers of the 16 Ferrero Rocher and place them in a small bag. Crush gently with a hammer or rolling pin, then set aside.

Place all the other ingredients in a large bowl and whisk vigorously with an electric whisk until totally combined and you have a thick texture. Using a spatula, stir in the crushed Ferrero Rocher. Pour into the prepared cake tin and bake for 45–50 minutes. Insert a toothpick to ensure the centre is cooked: if it emerges clean, the cake is ready. Transfer to a wire rack and allow to cool for at least 45 minutes.

For the topping, place the chocolate and cream in a medium heatproof bowl and melt over a small saucepan of simmering water (don't let the bowl touch the water). Using a spatula, stir continuously. Once all the chocolate has melted and combined with the cream, take the bowl off the saucepan. Using the spatula, or a palette knife, spread the chocolate topping over the cake, ensuring you cover both the top and sides. Place immediately in the fridge for 15 minutes to allow the topping to set.

Remove from the fridge, sprinkle the chopped hazelnuts on top and place 3 Ferrero Rochers in the centre. Honestly, heaven on a plate… And you're welcome x

SEMIFREDDO WITH HAZELNUT ICE CREAM AND CAKE

SPUMONI

◆◆◆◆◆◆◆◆◆◆◆◆◆◆◆◆◆◆◆◆◆◆◆◆

Ice cream, sponge cake, fruit and nuts – what is not to like in a dessert when you have all these ingredients combined? I made this for Jessica while touring through Puglia, and, as she was saying that no dessert could top the beautiful setting I had picked for us to enjoy this treat, a mouthful was taken and her eyes said it all. It's a fantastic dessert which can be made days before needed. Remember to take it out of the freezer for about five minutes before serving, to soften slightly.

SERVES 6–8

400g chocolate and hazelnut ice cream, softened

100g sponge cake, shop-bought is fine, cut to the size of the tin

30ml Amaretto liqueur

500ml double cream

200g condensed milk

finely grated zest of 1 orange (ideally unwaxed, if possible)

80g amarena cherries in syrup, drained, syrup reserved

50g roasted hazelnuts, crushed

1 tbsp finely chopped candied orange zest

Line a 900g loaf tin with cling film, making sure you have at least 10cm extra on each long side, so you can cover the top of the *spumoni*.

Spoon the ice cream into the prepared tin and use a spatula to level it out. Lay the piece of cake on top of the ice cream, gently pressing down. Drizzle over the Amaretto to soak into the sponge.

Whip the cream to soft peaks, then fold in the condensed milk, orange zest and cherries. Cover the sponge layer with the cream and fold over the cling film to cover. Place in the freezer for a minimum of 6 hours, or ideally overnight.

Remove the *spumoni* from the freezer about 5 minutes before you are ready to serve. Slice it into thick pieces and serve sprinkled with crushed roasted hazelnuts, some of the cherry syrup and the candied orange zest.

VANILLA AND CHOCOLATE MOUSSE

MOUSSE DI FIOCCHI DI CIOCCOLATO

◆◆◆◆◆◆◆◆◆◆◆◆◆◆◆◆◆◆◆◆◆◆◆◆◆

Over the years I have created lots of different chocolate mousses, flavoured with coffee, liqueurs, and even chilli, but when making a mousse for young children, milk chocolate always seems to be the winner. This recipe is so easy and only has four ingredients. You can substitute the chocolate bars for chocolate buttons, or, if you want a richer taste, just use 250g dark chocolate and no chocolate bars. Trust me: the kids or your dinner guests will love you forever with this dessert, and it takes no time at all to prepare.

SERVES 6

50g dark chocolate, 70% cocoa solids, broken into small pieces

8 x flaky milk chocolate bars (such as Flakes), broken into small pieces, plus 6 more to serve

500ml double cream

2 tsp vanilla extract

Place the dark chocolate, 8 chocolate bars and half the cream (250ml) in a medium heatproof bowl and melt over a small saucepan of simmering water (don't let the bowl touch the water). Using a spatula, stir continuously. Once all the chocolate has melted and combined with the cream, take the bowl off the saucepan, stir in the vanilla extract and set aside.

In the meantime, place the remaining cream in a separate bowl, and, using an electric whisk, whip it into medium peaks. Don't overwhip it, or the mousse will be too dense and not as airy.

Using a spatula, gently fold the chocolate mixture into the whipped cream.

Equally spoon the chocolate mousse into 6 martini glasses, or other glasses, or ramekins, of about 150ml capacity. Cover with cling film and place in the fridge for at least 1 hour.

When ready to serve, cut the remaining 6 chocolate bars in half. Crumble half a bar over each mousse. Insert the remaining half into the mousse and serve your chocolate heaven up to your family. Most children end up using the flaky chocolate bar as a spoon, some adults do too… I won't tell if you won't.

PANETTONE AND BUTTER PUDDING

TORTA SOFFICE CON PANETTONE E COINTREAU

◆◆◆◆◆◆◆◆◆◆◆◆◆◆◆◆◆◆◆◆◆◆◆◆◆

This has to be one of my all-time favourite desserts. It makes bread-and-butter pudding so easy, as the fruits are already in the cake. The rich flavours are enhanced by the Cointreau and creamy vanilla Custard (see page 240) balances the dish perfectly. I can eat this after any meal, no matter how full I am. If you prefer, substitute the Cointreau with brandy or Marsala wine.

SERVES 6

750ml whole milk

finely grated zest of 1 orange (ideally unwaxed, if possible)

50g salted butter, at room temperature

6 slices of panettone, each about 3cm thick

50g flaked almonds

3 eggs

50g caster sugar

30ml Cointreau

30g Demerara sugar

Custard (optional), to serve (see page 240)

In a medium saucepan, heat the milk with the orange zest and gently bring to the boil. Take off the heat and allow to rest.

Preheat the oven to 180°C/fan 160°C/Gas 4.

In the meantime, butter the slices of panettone and cut them into triangles.

Spread half the almonds out on the base of an ovenproof dish (about 25 x 20 x 8cm) and then neatly overlap the panettone triangles on top.

In a large bowl, beat the eggs, caster sugar and Cointreau together. Slowly pour in the orange-infused milk and mix well using a hand-held whisk.

Spoon the mixture over the sliced panettone and leave to soak for about 5 minutes. Using your fingers, gently push the panettone down into the milk mixture. If you have time, allow it to rest at this stage for 30 minutes.

Sprinkle the top with Demerara sugar, cover with foil and place in a roasting tin containing enough hot water to come halfway up the sides of the dish.

Bake in the oven for 35 minutes until the custard is lightly set. Remove the foil, sprinkle over the remaining almonds and bake for a final 20 minutes.

Serve up with a big spoon into warmed bowls and pour over home-made Custard or cream. Yum!

CUSTARD

CREMA PASTICCERA

◆◆◆◆◆◆◆◆◆◆◆◆◆◆◆◆◆◆◆◆◆◆◆◆◆◆◆◆

I know this isn't technically a dessert in its own right, but custard is just so perfect with so many desserts that it had to go into this chapter. I particularly recommend this with my Panettone and Butter Pudding (see page 238). People often worry about making custard themselves, in case it curdles, but honestly, follow this recipe and it will change your perception forever. Cool it down and use it for trifle, pour it over fresh fruit, or even just eat as is… once you have made your own custard, I promise you will never buy it again.

SERVES 6

4 large egg yolks
2 tbsp vanilla extract
60g caster sugar
2 tbsp cornflour
700ml whole milk
200ml double cream

Place the egg yolks, vanilla, sugar and cornflour in a medium bowl, and, using an electric whisk, whisk until pale. Set aside.

Pour the milk and cream into a medium saucepan and place over a medium heat. Very gently bring to just below boiling point. Basically, when you see a couple of bubbles forming, take the pan off the heat.

Pour the warmed creamed milk slowly into the beaten eggs, whisking continuously using a hand-held whisk. Once combined, pour back into the saucepan and place over a low heat.

Gently simmer, constantly stirring, until the custard thickens. How thick you want it is up to you, but I think cooking it for about 8 minutes is perfect, as longer than that can run the risk of curdling. If you are making this in advance, or wanting to serve the custard cold, take the saucepan off the heat and place a sheet of cling film on top (actually on top, touching the surface of the custard). This will ensure a skin does not form. Taste it. Told you: you will never buy custard again!

FRESH FRUIT HAZELNUT PAVLOVA

MERINGA CON FRUTTA FRESCA E NOCCIOLINE

◆◆◆◆◆◆◆◆◆◆◆◆◆◆◆◆◆◆◆◆◆◆◆◆◆◆◆◆

Fresh fruit pavlova is ultimately versatile. You can use seasonal fruits and be as creative as you like. I have added hazelnuts to this meringue to give it more texture, but, of course, if you are allergic to nuts, or prefer a traditional pavlova, just eliminate them. Be really gentle when putting the cream on top, but don't panic if it all breaks, you can just make an Eton Mess instead!

SERVES 8–10

FOR THE PAVLOVA
6 large egg whites
350g caster sugar
2 tsp vanilla extract
50g chopped hazelnuts
1 tsp white wine vinegar
2 tsp cornflour

FOR THE TOPPING
300ml whipping cream
1 tbsp vanilla extract
12 strawberries, hulled and halved
12 raspberries
20 blackberries
2 kiwi fruit, peeled and finely sliced
handful of blueberries

Preheat the oven to 180°C/fan 160°C/Gas 4.

Line a baking tray with non-stick baking parchment and draw a rectangle on it about 30 x 20cm, or, if you prefer a round pavlova, then draw a 25cm diameter circle.

Place the egg whites in a large bowl and whisk with an electric whisk until stiff peaks are formed. Pour in half the sugar and whisk again until the mixture is thick and glossy. Using a spatula, fold in the remaining sugar, the vanilla, nuts, vinegar and cornflour.

Spoon the meringue on to the baking sheet, following your chosen shape. Form higher peaks at the edges and try and make the centre as flat as possible.

Place in the middle of the oven and bake for 5 minutes, then reduce the oven temperature to 140°C/fan 120°C/Gas 1 and continue to cook for a further 1 hour. Turn the oven off. Leave the meringue to cool completely in the oven for at least 3 hours, or even overnight.

Pour the cream and vanilla extract into a medium bowl and whip with an electric whisk until soft peaks are formed.

Gently dollop the vanilla cream mixture into the centre of the meringue, spreading it out gently to the sides and leaving a border of about 2cm clear. Decorate with the fruit and serve.

THANK YOU

GRAZIE

◆◆◆◆◆◆◆◆◆◆◆◆◆◆◆◆◆◆◆◆◆◆◆◆◆◆◆◆◆

I dedicate this book to my mother Alba and father Ciro. They are missed every day, but the whole family felt the loss of their presence during filming and collating the D'Acampo's favourite recipes. Their love for life, family and food will live forever in my heart and I promise to instil it in all future D'Acampos!

I would like to start by thanking my agent Matt Kay (also known as Jerry Maguire) for his continued friendship and support. Thank you to all at Studio Ramsay for their hard work, dedication and vision on the production, and to ITV, for continuing to believe in me to do another food project, and this time allowing my family to be included, banking those special memories we all live for!

Grazie to my beautiful country, Italy, for always receiving me with love, warmth and great food. Everyone I ever encounter on my journeys through the regions of the country always welcomes me with open arms and a great espresso and I am forever grateful.

Thank you to all at Bloomsbury Publishing. A special mention to Rowan Yapp, Lena Hall, Laura Brodie in Production, Don Shanahan in Marketing and Sarah Bennie in PR. We have a fantastic partnership and I am really looking forward to creating many more books together. Thanks to Mark Arn, Gillian Powell-Tuck and Ash Jordan for the lovely design, to Liz Haarala and Max Hamilton for the stunning photos, and to Dinah Drazin for getting it all on to the pages with such elan. A huge thank you to Lucy Bannell, my editor, who kept my spellings and grammar intact as well as much more.

Thank you, and much love always, to Abbi Rose for being my right-hand girl on every shoot and for continuing to make me (and on this occasion, all the family) look half-decent!

To my beautiful family, Jessica my wife, and my amazing children, Luciano, Rocco and Mia. You are my world and I love you all so much. Big kisses and cuddles to my mother and father-in-law, Elizabeth and Malcolm de Friend, so glad I got to spend some special quality time with you both. Thank you for always being there for me.

Finally, thanks to all of you. Thank you for laughing with me, supporting me and encouraging me to do better by always trying to create more recipes for you to try. You are always on my journeys and will continue to be my inspiration. I cannot tell you how much I appreciate you all — thank you from the bottom of my heart.

INDEX

INDICE

◆◆◆◆◆◆◆◆◆◆◆◆◆◆◆◆◆◆◆◆◆◆◆◆◆◆◆

◆◆◆◆◆◆◆◆◆◆◆◆◆◆◆◆◆◆◆◆◆◆◆◆◆◆◆

◆◆◆◆◆◆◆◆◆◆◆◆◆◆◆◆◆◆◆◆◆◆◆

◆◆◆◆◆◆◆◆◆◆◆◆◆◆◆◆◆◆◆◆◆◆◆◆◆◆◆

◆◆◆◆◆◆◆◆◆◆◆◆◆◆◆◆◆◆◆◆◆◆◆◆◆

◆◆◆◆◆◆◆◆◆◆◆◆◆◆◆◆◆◆◆◆◆◆◆◆◆◆

BLOOMSBURY PUBLISHING
Bloomsbury Publishing Plc
50 Bedford Square, London WC1B 3DP, UK
29 Earlsfort Terrace, Dublin 2, Ireland

BLOOMSBURY, BLOOMSBURY PUBLISHING and the Diana logo are
trademarks of Bloomsbury Publishing Plc

First published in Great Britain in 2021
Text © Gino D'Acampo 2021

Photographs © HaaralaHamilton 2021

Photographs on pages 21 and 246 © Conor O'Leary 2021

The information contained in this book is provided by way of general guidance in relation to the specific subject
matters addressed herein, but it is not a substitute for specialist dietary advice. It should not be relied on for
medical, health-care, pharmaceutical or other professional advice on specific dietary or health needs. This book
is sold with the understanding that the author and publisher are not engaged in rendering medical, health or
any other kind of personal or professional services. The reader should consult a competent medical or health
professional before adopting any of the suggestions in this book or drawing inferences from it.

A catalogue record for this book is available from the British Library

ISBN: HB 978-1-5266-2831-2; eBook 978-1-5266-2832-9

2 4 6 8 10 9 7 5 3 1

Project Editor: Lucy Bannell
Designer: Superfantastic
Interior Layouts: Dinah Drazin
Photographer: HaaralaHamilton
Food Stylist: Claire Bassano
Prop Stylist: Jennifer Kay
Indexer: Vanessa Bird
Printed and bound in Germany by Mohn Media

To find out more about our authors and books visit www.bloomsbury.com and sign up for our newsletters